ISBN 978-0-282-56562-6
PIBN 10857111

# 1 MONTH OF
# FREE
# READING

## at

## www.ForgottenBooks.com

By purchasing this book you are eligible for one month membership to ForgottenBooks.com, giving you unlimited access to our entire collection of over 700,000 titles via our web site and mobile apps.

To claim your free month visit: www.forgottenbooks.com/free857111

English
Français
Deutsche
Italiano
Español
Português

# www.forgottenbooks.com

**Mythology** Photography **Fiction**
Fishing Christianity **Art** Cooking
Essays Buddhism Freemasonry
Medicine **Biology** Music **Ancient
Egypt** Evolution Carpentry Physics
Dance Geology **Mathematics** Fitness
Shakespeare **Folklore** Yoga Marketing
**Confidence** Immortality Biographies
Poetry **Psychology** Witchcraft
Electronics Chemistry History **Law**
Accounting **Philosophy** Anthropology
Alchemy Drama Quantum Mechanics
Atheism Sexual Health **Ancient History**
**Entrepreneurship** Languages Sport
Paleontology Needlework Islam
**Metaphysics** Investment Archaeology
Parenting Statistics Criminology
**Motivational**

*Dedicated to*

*Bernard & Ines Burrows*

# ACKNOWLEDGMENTS

To the following, acknowledgments are due for permission to quote poems and extracts:

Messrs. Chatto & Windus for lines from the poetry of Wilfred Owen.

The Clarendon Press, Oxford, for lines from *The Shorter Poems of Robert Bridges.*

Mrs. W. H. Davies and Jonathan Cape Ltd., for lines from *The Collected Poems of W. H. Davies.*

Mr. Walter de la Mare, Mr. Siegfried Sassoon, Mr. Stephen Spender and Messrs. Faber & Faber, Ltd.

Mrs. Helen Thomas for a poem by Edward Thomas.

Mrs. W. B. Yeats and Macmillan & Co. Ltd., for a poem from *Collected Poems of W. B. Yeats.*

# CONTENTS

*By the same author*

NOVELS
*Panic Spring*
*Cefalu*
*The Black Book*
*Prospero's Cell*

POETRY
*A Private Country*
*Cities, Plains and People*
*On Seeming to Presume*
*Sappho: a Play*

# PREFACE

THIS book, now divided for the sake of convenience into essays, is not one which I would have written for choice. It was composed and delivered as a series of lectures on modern poetry during the course of my duties as a lecturer in English Literature attached to the British Council in Argentina during 1948. The present text, which has hardly been altered at all, is what typographers would call a 'mock-up' for the lectures which were designed to appeal to an audience of graduate teachers in English, gathered from the various universities of Argentina.

The object of the exercise was a double one: first to supply a satisfactory key to the complexities of contemporary practice in poetry, and secondly to give a brief account of the poets writing today. The limitations of this book, then, should be judged in the light of these objectives. If I have been in danger of over-simplifying ideas in the introductory passages, and of dealing too briefly with important writers in the guide, it is because I had to make both the key and the guide fit into the narrow compass of ten lectures.

If most writing about modern poetry is apologetic the reason is clear to see. The unspoken question at the back of the common reader's mind today is always: 'Why doesn't the poet say what he means more clearly?' The conviction that modern poetry is something incredibly difficult and arcane is perhaps excusable. During the last twenty years we have seen barbarities of technique and curiosities of form which would be enough to frighten and displease the most well-disposed of readers. Who can blame the poor literature teacher for stopping short at Hardy's later lyrics and refusing to penetrate any further into the contemporary jungle? A few of the bolder spirits have tip-toed forward in the direction of Sir Henry Newbolt and the early de La Mare, but they soon take fright when they reach the great moat which T. S. Eliot has dug between the Georgian stockades and the poetry of the late twenties. The problem of modern verse is one which faces the common reader no less than the common student, and the publication of this book rests upon the belief that a new line of attack is necessary and possible for those who want to cross the great divide which separates a poem like *The Hound of Heaven* from *The Waste Land* or *Ulysses* from *Gerontion*.

Wilde says somewhere that one of the most effective ways of hating art is to admire it rationally: and this is true. So many critics and lecturers in this domain cut up their subject and anatomize it rationally—that in the end it tastes like an apple cut with a steel knife. My object here was not to provide good and rational reasons for liking modern work; but simply to help my students (and now, I hope, the common reader to whom this book is addressed) to clear away much of the pedagogic lumber which accumulates insensibly in minds brought up in the traditions of scientific rationalism. In order to clear the approaches to poetry something like a brief disintoxication course is needed. The problem is, in some sort, how to persuade people to become their own contemporaries. To this end I have tried to set out, not according to rigid pattern but haphazardly, a few of the influences of the age, picking up now a theory from psycho-analysis, now a hypothesis from modern physics. Deficient in true scholarship, I have been able to bring to the job only a wide if haphazard reading, and enough practice in writing poetry to have learned to distrust everybody's theories about it: my own most of all. Nevertheless I count it as part of the success of these lectures that where I did not get a student to accept my views I did at least drive him distractedly in the direction of wider reading and bolder association of ideas, which often ended in him developing views which were truly his own. I take this to be the only measure of real success by which a lecturer can judge the quality of his materials and the density of his own thoughts.

'I am rather induced to set down the history of arts as a species of natural history,' says Bacon, 'because it is the fashion to talk as if art were something different from nature, so that things artificial should be separated from things natural, as differing totally in kind.' I have thought to present poetry as one dialect of a greater language comprising the whole universe of ideas—a universe perpetually shifting, changing its relations and tenses as verbs do in speech, altering its outlines. By this means I hoped to trap those qualities which were inherent in the poets of a given time, and which may be inferred by their technical approach to the subject-matter in hand.

For us, in this time, the cardinal points of attack upon the sensibilities of the average reader seem to me to lie between the new hypotheses concerning the self or psyche, and the new theories about the make-up of the universe we are inhabiting. Psychology and anthropology have both offered tempting ports of call, though I have been content to spend in either case only a few hours ashore. Science is a continent rather than a country. I have tried to point to a loosening of links in the deterministic chain as the most interesting thing about it today.

Wherever possible I have tried to quote from books which were or are readily accessible in cheap editions, bearing in mind that the student is usually as poor as his teacher; while at the time these lectures were composed Argentina was suffering from the post-war shortage of books which afflicted so many European countries and which, even today, is not quite banished.

Of the books which have helped me to formulate some of my own vague ideas about literature two should be of interest to all students of the contemporary scene: Wyndham Lewis' *Time and Western Man* and Edmund Wilson's *Axel's Castle*. It will not be difficult to pick out the ideas I have derived from these two admirable surveys. As for the main bias of my own thinking (if I may, for want of a better word, call it that), it has developed out of a study of anthropologists like Tylor, Frazer, Rivers, etc.: of psychologists like Jung, Rank, Groddeck and their great master, Freud: of scientists like Eddington, Whitehead and Einstein. I have always regarded these various fields of thought as interlocking and mutually fertilizing, and have never hesitated to borrow an idea from one to apply in another. But such originality as this book possesses lies only in the arrangement of the material—not in the factual comprehensiveness of its demonstration. It is a sketch for a Method—not a painting in oils.

Meanwhile, of course, poetry is there in the shadows, secure from our definitions and explanations, in appearance an almost autonomous faculty, in operation posing as communication. To those who practise her she appears ennobling and exasperating; to those who read her a mad nymph locked in a prism; to those who preach about her (too often alas) a butterfly pinned to a cork slab and classified. As for the poet, he is a child of nature and would agree with Bacon that 'Nature to be commanded must be obeyed;' and 'that which in contemplation is as the cause, is in operation as the rule.'

In conclusion, I am bound to thank the British Council for permission to reprint these lectures, the composition of which helped me to pass away a year in an uncongenial climate to our mutual profit. A few brief notes, at the end, are signalled in the text of the first four chapters by an asterisk.

Oxford,
1952.

## CHAPTER I

# THE LIMITS OF CRITICISM

> Out of these tensions a unique literature has arisen, abnormally difficult to assess, irresistibly fascinating to study. Will it prove to be merely the record of unco-ordinated efforts? Not unless we expect a conventional progress along academic lines, easily divisible into types and schools. Instead of such conformity we shall find guesses, adventures, experiments which seem at first to be irresponsible, but gradually acquire a common spirit of discovery peculiar to the age. . . . That is why the study of twentieth-century literature is inseparable from the study of ideas.
>
> H. V. ROUTH
> *English Literature and Ideas in the Twentieth Century*

IT would not be fair to embark upon a series of lectures concerned with modern poetry without first trying to indicate ·a few of the major limitations of critical method. That they are not always obvious to those who talk about literature is clear from the habits of so many lecturers who tend to discuss literature in terms of itself so to speak instead of in terms of the age which produced it. Now if we are to consider poetry as something self-contained, something which cannot be referred to other departments of human thought, we will be doing it a disservice as critics, for literature is only one facet of the prism which we call culture. All the arts and sciences are simply different dialects of the same language, all contributing towards an attitude to life. What is this 'culture'? I take this word to mean the sum, at any given time, of all the efforts man is making to interpret the universe about him. Ideas from the various departments of thought cross-fertilize each other, and it is sometimes a good idea to discuss one kind of thought in terms of another. We will never, of course, succeed in fully defining a given culture for that would mean becoming fully conscious of it—and a culture dies when it becomes conscious of itself.

Today all the arts and sciences seem to be differentiated from one another, but this is really an illusion born of faulty critical method. In ancient Greece mathematics, music, poetry and sculpture were intimately connected and the systems of education then in vogue recognized the fact. Today we still acknowledge this underground connection between the arts and sciences when we find ourselves using phrases like 'a man of his age' or 'the prevailing currents of thought'.

It is easy enough to see that even today the arts are permeated by mathematical ideas: architecture and sculpture are still second-cousins to mathematical theory, while music and metre betray their relation to mathematical quantity. So it is that when you look at the art of an epoch in any of its modes you see that, taken in the round, it constitutes a cosmology, an overall interpretation of the universe we inhabit.

Now the difficulty of all criticism, of all interpretation, whether of a work of art or of a system of scientific ideas, is the subjective element. Human beings suffer from binocular vision: if you look at the stars through a pair of binoculars you can only see a small part of the sky at once. The act of thinking about something creates a field around the object observed, and in order to think about that object you must neglect the whole from which the object has been separated. It is easy to see what a grave limitation this is, particularly for a critic. Everything is part of some greater whole. Everything is the sum of smaller parts. How, then, can we deal with the object-in-itself?

Let me give you an analogy from the naturalist's world to illustrate this dependence—this relation of one idea to the whole body of thought. There is an organism which

2

floats about in the Gulf Stream, called the *siphnophora*.* It can be found as a single cell and also as a large cluster of cells. Now this is the curious thing about it: the single cell is a complete animal, equipped with digestive apparatus, entire unto itself. However when several thousand of these cells join up they undergo a radical modification and become parts of an equally entire but much larger animal. Some of the single cells take on the work of the digestive apparatus, some shape themselves into an alimentary tract, and so on. Soon there is only one big animal, and no trace of the individuals composing it. So it is with ideas, and with the words we use to express them. Existing singly, they also have the power to modify, and form greater wholes in other contexts.

I do not think I need to remind you how in every age the great conceptual abstractions like 'truth', 'beauty' and 'eternity' have been discussed and examined and defined: without any final judgment being reached upon them. For our purposes we might as well label these great abstractions 'irreducible quantities'. The materials we use for thinking are so unstable that it is unlikely we shall ever reach a final definition, a final judgment upon them. Yet we are forced to use them. There is no final truth to be found —there is only provisional truth within a given context.

I mention these facts, not because I do not think you are aware of them, but in order to make my own position clear. To lecture about reality is to stop it—as one might stop a film—and lecture about the still image of reality instead: the still picture upon the screen. That is the most thought can do. It is not a very encouraging position for the critic to find himself in, but we must accept it. Reason is only a trusted middleman in the commerce between logic and illumination. We should be careful to treat it as a friend without letting it become a tyrant.

Much has been thought and written about poetry since Aristotle and yet today we are still in the position of

3

Madame Rimbaud with regard to it. You will remember that she was the first member of the general public to see *La Saison en Enfer*. 'What does it mean?' she said angrily. To which her son replied as angrily: 'It means exactly what it says.' In other words he had chosen that means of expression, because it seemed to him to convey his own meaning in the most exact way. We must accept the poet's word order as the clearest statement of what he means. To explain a work of art takes us unfortunately further away from its real meaning—which the sensibility will recognize as a whole, not as a series of parts. We must keep this in mind, too, when we come to think as critics.

Then again, among the great unknowns which form the boundaries to our lives both physical and spiritual, there stands death. While we are sitting here he is advancing upon us at the rate of sixty seconds to the minute, sixty minutes to the hour. Of course this is a purely human measurement of death. For all we know he may move much faster or slower. Time is the measure of our death-consciousness. There are other organisms, we know, which measure time by a heat-unit. They must have a different idea of death. Then there are those so-called simple cells which multiply by binary fission—they simply divide into two. You might say one dies into two, leaving no corpse behind it as a human being does. Does the caterpillar die to become a moth or would you call it being born? We do not know. In some cases birth and death would seem to be almost interchangeable terms.

If you turn to modern astronomy you will find that the measurement of distances has so far outrun the scale of human calculations that we are using a composite word 'light-years' as a unit of time and space. Time has extended itself almost beyond comprehension.

If we live in a very special relation to time it is perhaps because within ourselves we realize that time is only a kind of death-measurement. I do not have to quote you

4

examples from poetry of this association. You find it everywhere. No sooner does the poet hear his wrist-watch ticking than he remembers that it is imitating his heart-beats, and that when they stop his life will be over. Anthropologists tell us that the sources of art lie in our immortality-wish and our fear of death, but pretty as the idea is it has the air of being an over-simplification. I do not think that the mystery of the creative act is so easily reducible to a formula, but this is a question each must decide for himself.

Man, says the philosopher, as soon as he noticed the irreversibility of process in the natural world, became afraid and decided to invent a way of circumventing death. It is certainly true that a cell multiplies and forms a plant: that the plant grows into a tree: that the tree dies and disintegrates. It is even more true that so far we have found no way of halting this process in nature—the stream of time which flows always one way, towards dissolution and death. I suspect that we would willingly surrender much of our art and science to find out what happens after death.

Meanwhile, of course, our observations are dogged by the subjective element. Man is simply a box labelled personality. He peers out of the box through five slits, the senses. On this earth he is permitted access to three dimensions of space and one of time. Only in his imagination can he inhabit the whole—a reality which is beyond the reach of intellectual qualification: a reality which even the greatest art is incapable of rendering in its full grandeur. It is a ridiculous and humiliating situation but we must accept it, and be content with our provisional truths, our short-range raids on this greater territory which permeates our inner lives—and which we try to avoid realizing behind the barriers of habit and laziness. If art has any message it must be this: to remind us that we are dying without having properly lived.

How to begin living, then? But this is another question, the answer to which lies not in art or science but in ourselves.

Next in the catalogue of limitations comes the relation between thought and feeling. They have never been successfully worked out either in terms of psychology or in terms of physiology. Presumably they never will be. I am reminded in this context of a phrase of Proust's which forms part of his description of an artist at work. He says:

> The effort made by Elstir to strip himself, when face to face with reality, of every intellectual concept, was all the more admirable in that this man, who before sitting down to paint made himself deliberately ignorant, forgot in his honesty of purpose everything he knew—since what one knows ceases to exist by itself.

*What one knows ceases to exist by itself!* The phrase is worth thinking over. What does it mean? That knowledge, thinking, only delimits the object, frames it, reduces its value as a Wholeness. Thinking limits the function of the thing to the power of the system within which it operates. The artist, then, does not exactly think while he works. He uses the ratiocinative side of himself only when he comes to arrange and edit what he has written or painted. The direct inspiration comes from somewhere else. From where? We do not know. And so far I have never seen any satisfactory account given by an artist which clears up this mystery. Most great artists appear to disclaim any responsibility for their work. It arrives from nowhere, they tell us. Their poems are written for them by the planchette.

Now if I am emphasizing the darkness that lies over the landscape of ideas it is because I want you to regard any ideas I put before you as provisional, as products of my peculiar temperament. I believe that a good critic should avoid the sin of a closed system: and if these lectures have the air of systematized arrangement it is because criticism

demands an appearance of order in its method. Nevertheless they should be labelled 'provisional hypotheses'. I am
anxious to avoid the dangers inherent in thinking along
straight lines in a universe which science tells us is curved.

If we are to think of the literature of our own age we
should choose some convenient point of departure. Of
course the whole content of a work of art is beyond simple
understanding by the head. The heaviest impact of the
work of art is in the guts. Art does not reason. It man-
handles you and changes you. But the artist is often
dependent on the armature of philosophic ideas or religious concepts, and we can sometimes surprise his intentions if we examine them. Art, after all, belongs to its age.
Indeed the greatest art creates its own age.

The chief characteristic of art today, if we are to judge
by the reactions of the common man, is its obscurity.
Everybody complains about obscurity in poetry, in painting, in music. I do not suggest that in some cases the com-
plaint is unjustified. But we should remember that the
really original work of art in any age seems obscure to the
general public. From a certain point of view it would be
true to say that no great work of art finds an appreciative
public waiting for it. The work creates its own public,
slowly and painfully. A work of art is born as an intellectual foundling. What is interesting to notice is that
often the art-specialists themselves are caught napping. It
was André Gide, you remember, who first saw Proust's
great novel while he was working as a reader for a firm of
publishers. He turned it down without any hesitation.
Perhaps you remember Leigh Hunt's verdict on Blake
as 'an unfortunate madman whose mildness alone prevented him from being locked up'. Wordsworth also
thought Blake mad, and yet it was he who wrote: 'Every
great and original writer, in proportion as he is great and
original, must himself create the taste by which he is to
be judged.'

Perhaps, however, the obscurity and difficulty of modern poetry might be better understood if we could discover its pedigree among the ideas which have influenced the contemporary artist. What are they? Let us mark off a piece of the historical time-track and see whether we cannot establish some significant relationships within the margin of, say, a hundred years. If we spread out the events and ideas of this period—if we sift out the gravel and examine one or two of the heavier objects which remain in the sieve we might reach a few conclusions, however tentative. Of course to use the historical method often leads one into over-simplifications—but you have been warned of these already.

To try and draw the family tree of the contemporary artist is not by any means an easy matter. It is like drawing a map of the Gulf Stream. It is quite easy to mark out the greater currents and to plot the general direction of their movements, but we would not be surprised to discover that within the greater currents there were cross-currents and even counter-currents flowing in arbitrary directions. This is where the critic gets cold feet and with reason. But there is no help for it—he must embark on his journey in the cockle-shell of thought, prepared for a stormy passage.

But in order to bring the subject of this enquiry down to laboratory level let me provide you with a couple of corpses to dissect. I have chosen two poems, one written in 1840 or thereabouts, and the other in 1920. Both are famous anthology pieces, and they are probably well known to you. If you lay them side by side you will at once notice a remarkable thing. They are all but identical in subject-matter. Both are written in the first person singular. Both present a sort of autobiography through the lips of an old man, a hero, who sits before his house, thinking about death. The similarity of the poems is indeed so striking that we could hardly select anything better to study. Would it be possible, by making use of the sharply contrasted material and style of these two poems, to risk a rash judgment about the world of 1840 as compared with that of 1920? Could the change of values between the two be traced which, so to speak, modified the subject matter of the first poem and allowed it to become the second? It would be worth trying perhaps.

The first of the poems is *Ulysses* by Lord Tennyson, the second is *Gerontion* by T. S. Eliot. In either case we have an old man's reflections upon past life and approaching death. Would it be stretching a point to consider the first as the hero of the Victorian Age and the second as the contemporary hero? I think not. Examined in the light of this idea the similarities between the two are almost as exciting as the differences. Both demonstrate the autobiographical method. Both present one with a definite attitude to life and to death. Both sum up the views of an old hero upon the age he represents.

Tennyson's broad classical manner and his simple syntax stand for a world of clear thinking and precise relations. Eliot's hero, however, allows the contents of memory and reflection to pass through him and emerge in a series of oracular statements, often apparently without any form and with only a superficial resemblance to grammatical proportion. *Gerontion* is rather like a series of ticker-tape messages coming in from some remote stock-room, and being recorded haphazardly one after the other. Memory, reflections, desire—they all seem inextricably tangled up, and in order to sort them out we shall have to do far more work than would be necessary to reduce and understand the content of *Ulysses*.

But leave the technical aspect on one side for a moment and let us see what differences exist between the actual things said by the two old men. How does the attitude of Gerontion differ from that of Ulysses? The most obvious difference seem to be between Ulysses' activity, his masterful bearing in the face of time, and Gerontion's passivity.

9

Gerontion is a victim. Ulysses is still the master of his fate. He dominates his world—that grave classical world which was founded upon the idealism and classicism of the Victorians. Bravery, nobility, dignity are the keynotes to his attitude. Gerontion shares none of these qualities. 'Here I am,' he says, 'an old man in a dry month, being read to by a boy, waiting for rain.' He disclaims any right to be considered a hero. If there were any great battles, he did not see them: 'I was neither at the hot gates nor fought in the warm rain nor knee-deep in the salt marsh, heaving a cutlass, bitten by flies, fought.'

Ulysses seems to have escaped the disillusion of Gerontion. His hunger is for more life: 'Life piled on life were all too little,' he says, and adds: 'All times I have enjoy'd greatly, have suffer'd greatly . . . I cannot rest from travel: I will drink life to the lees.' Gerontion, however, replies to this: 'I have lost my passion: why should I need to keep it since what is kept must be adulterated?'

Ulysses feels a part of the historic fabric: 'I am become a name . . . much have I seen and known; cities of men and manners, climates, councils, governments, myself not least, but honour'd of them all.' He is not proud or complacent. He is simply fully aware of himself and alive at all points. Gerontion on the other hand has no such sense of himself as a part of historic progress: 'History has many cunning passages,' he whines, 'contrived corridors and issues, de-ceives with whispering ambitions, guides us by vanities . . . gives when our attention is distracted . . . Gives too late what's not believed in, or if, still believed, in memory only, reconsidered passion.' History, then, is for him something that deludes and tricks. His voice is the voice of someone who has been deceived by the world, let down by it. Ulysses has faced and dominated it.

As for knowledge, the contrast in attitude between the two old men is even more definite. Ulysses' 'grey spirit yearning in desire to follow knowledge, like a sinking star,

beyond the utmost bound of human thought' is matched
by the question of Gerontion: 'After such knowledge, what
forgiveness? . . . We have not reached conclusion, when I
stiffen in a rented house.' He cannot bring himself to
exclaim, as Ulysses does: ' 'Tis not too late to seek a newer
world.' For Gerontion the boundaries of human thought
and hope have narrowed down to these 'thoughts of a dry
brain in a dry season'. The thoughts of an old man 'driven
by the Trades to a sleepy corner'. In the face of the Greek
heroism and daring of Ulysses he can only mutter:

> Think
> Neither fear nor courage saves us. Unnatural vices
> Are fathered by our heroism. Virtues
> Are forced upon us by our impudent crimes.
> These tears are shaken from the wrath-bearing tree.

I have said enough to show, I hope, that we are faced by
a tremendous difference in values when we consider these
two poems side by side. Something radical seems to have
happened to the hero's idea of himself between 1840 and
1920. History might be able to offer us some clues.

Now if we re-read *Gerontion* with half the attention that
a company director gives to a stock-report we may be able
to trace other preoccupations. You must not imagine, however, that I am attempting any very profound analysis of
this fine poem. I have ignored the technical and linguistic
features of it for the time being. Later I hope to discuss
why Gerontion speaks as he does. But for the moment it is
enough to consider the poem as a piece of simple autobiography, and to try and find out a bit more of the circumstances of Gerontion's life. His speech is rather difficult
to follow at times but he does seem to imply a number of
things about himself that are worth our attention.

You have seen how securely grounded in his world
Ulysses is. He does not, to give one example, fear for the
succession of his son. He is simply bored with old age,

bored with the inactivity he is forced to endure. He longs to resume his youthful, adventurous life.

What of Gerontion? 'My house,' he says, 'is a decayed house, and the jew squats on the window sill, the owner.' Later on in the poem he mentions that it is a rented house. We know that house as a symbol stands for more than four walls and a roof. A house means property, succession, home and family order. It also, by association, stands for children. Surely we may read into this passage a pre-occupation with the break-up of a social order, together with a far-reaching sense of insecurity about the values upon which that order was once founded.

> Signs are taken for wonders. 'We would see a sign!'
> The word within a word, unable to speak a word,
> Swaddled with darkness. In the juvescence of the year
> Came Christ the tiger.

It is revelation and not more knowledge that Gerontion appears to be waiting for; later comes the phrase 'to be eaten, to be divided, to be drunk' and it reminds us of the Christian sacrament. Yet with a sudden ironic turn Eliot brings before us a gallery of *personae* such as one might only see in some small Florentine pension, or perhaps in a Bloomsbury boarding-house for foreign students. 'Mr. Silvero . . . who walked all night in the next room; by Hakagawa, bowing among the Titians'. These, he seems to say, are the creatures for whom Christ commanded his sacrament to be conducted. They are mere shadows of men he has met on his travels. Yet these figures are to Gerontion what the 'peers' of Ulysses were once. 'The great Achilles' and the rest. They are mythological shapes which inhabit the subjective world of Gerontion. Ulysses and Achilles were world-figures. They belonged to racial myth. But the myth is dead and for Gerontion only these deper-sonalized masks remain in his memory.

Something very mysterious has happened to the firm

classical order of things, and to the heroic nature of man. In Gerontion everything seems to be called into question, not only the doctrine of his age but the knowledge, the morals and, on the social plane, the security of family life and natural succession. 'I have no ghosts,' he says. As the poem progresses in its unformal yet rhythmical way you begin to realize that it expresses a very deep-seated sense of insecurity and intellectual exhaustion, together with a strong condemnation of the moral order under which the modern hero has to live. History leads nowhere. Human identity seems to be empty of any joy. Compare these statements, with their mounting flavour of disenchantment, with the marvellous closing lines of *Ulysses* which express faith and affirmation in the human condition:

> The long day wanes: the slow moon climbs: the deep
> Moans round with many voices. Come, my friends,
> 'Tis not too late to seek a newer world.
> Push off, and sitting well in order smite
> The sounding furrows; for my purpose holds
> To sail beyond the sunset, and the baths
> Of all the western stars, until I die.
> It may be that the gulfs will wash us down:
> It may be we shall touch the Happy Isles,
> And see the great Achilles, whom we knew.
> Tho' much is taken, much abides; and tho'
> We are not now that strength which in old days
> Moved earth and heaven; that which we are, we are;
> One equal temper of heroic hearts,
> Made weak by time and fate, but strong in will
> To strive, to seek, to find, and not to yield.

*Gerontion*, however, ends very much as it began. 'Thoughts of a dry brain in a dry season.' There is no way forward, the poem says, after it has enumerated those thoughts of a dry brain. Gerontion is in an intellectual *impasse*. He cannot advance. He can only sit and think of the past until his memories

Protract the profit of their chilled delirium,
Excite the membrane, when the sense has cooled,
With pungent sauces, multiply variety
In a wilderness of mirrors.

What is the secret of this loss of faith, of this negation?
You may perhaps think that in putting such a question I
am taking unpardonable liberties with my material. Who
can say whether the difference in the two poems does not
reflect purely temperamental idiosyncrasies? Tennyson
was a hero-worshipper, while T. S. Eliot was, at the time
he wrote *Gerontion*, a cynic. There may be something to be
said for this view. Obviously temperament and subject-
matter play a very important part in the poems. Yet if
poems reflect their age at all we may be able to dig under
the surface for their cosmological content, and leave the
personal data to look after itself. It is certainly true that
the later poems of Tennyson also became pessimistic—yet
the gap between his technique and that of Eliot remains as
wide. Can we trace historic origins for the change? Can
we, by following up the changes of thought and belief
within the last hundred years, find some sort of clue to the
exhausted subjectivity of the contemporary hero? I think
we can.

The problem is where to begin—for both in the arts and
sciences the last hundred years has been one of the most
momentous epochs in human history. Between 1840 and
1900 lie sixty years characterized by tremendous intellectual upheavals, tremendous changes in beliefs and values.
Let us take a simple example.

The Victorians believed, among other things, that time
had begun less than 6,000 years ago. Moses, they thought,
was only separated from the first man by a few generations.
In the Bampton Lecture of 1859 George Rawlinson
gravely suggested that Moses' mother, Jochebed, had probably met Jacob who could have known Noah's son Shem.
Shem was probably acquainted with Methuselah, who

had been for 243 years a contemporary of Adam. Adam himself had been made on the sixth day after the beginning of Time. The earth, according to the Victorians, had been created about 4,000 B.C. by God, and was more or less as we see it today, except that the perfect life we had been meant to lead on it had been corrupted by the Fall.

It is very hard to put ourselves in the position of people who believed this sort of thing. For us geology tells a different story. But geology is a science still in its infancy. When it first arose and questioned the facts of *Genesis* the assertions made by its followers seemed positively blasphemous. Yet its assertions gained ground. It became obvious that the account of creation given in *Genesis* would not bear close examination. The shock was a considerable one, and the whole age was filled with clamouring voices, with quarrels and speculations centring about the discoveries of geology. In 1857 the first remains of Neanderthal Man came to light. Then came the publication of Darwin's *Origin of Species* which made man, not the noblest member of the animal kingdom but simply a term in the evolutionary series. This idea caused perhaps the greatest shock of all. It was, needless to say, most bitterly contested both from inside the Church and from outside it. Yet the effect of this idea upon the Victorian Age cannot be overestimated. Man had been dethroned. He was no longer the noblest animal. Sherwood Taylor in a recent article on the beliefs of the Victorian Age* says:

> For lack of clear thinking in these matters many lost their faith completely. Some felt that the historicity of the scriptural Adam was overthrown, and the doctrine of the fall and the need for redemption with it: and so came to lose belief in the Christian scheme. Others felt that the Bible had been shown to be untrue in some points and therefore no longer carried any assurance of authenticity. . . . I myself have little doubt that in England it was geology and the theory of evolution that changed us from a Christian to a pagan nation.

15

The overt reaction of the age to geology was theological but its influence extended to every phase of thought. It completed in fact the revolution that Copernicus began.

The history of man, then, was suddenly expanded into a region of time so remote that the Victorians might be forgiven for finding the idea terrifying. Lyell, the greatest geologist, suggested that man was 100,000 years old. When you think that the art and morality of Europe were based upon the Bible you can imagine how deep a shock all this was. But it was not all.

History began to expand in another direction, helped this time by archaeology. In 1874 Schliemann's excavations at Mycenae were begun. You will remember that the poems of Homer were considered mere poetical fantasies. Schliemann was later to prove that Troy existed. In 1895 Sir Flinders Petrie was at work upon ancient remains in Egypt, while in 1899 Sir Arthur Evans began work upon what was to turn out to be a new civilization, until then unknown, called the Minoan civilization. Ancient cultures were coming to the surface, and the chill wind of religious scepticism was blowing hard. First it was the civilization of Europe which began to look remote and tiny set against the historical perspectives opened up. Secondly the history of man on earth, as explained by geologists, began to appear of negligible importance.

In 1897, in an essay upon literature, Professor J. W. Hales wrote:

> Science has certainly been in part responsible for the growth of a spirit of materialism, and has caused those who do not share that spirit to examine themselves and remould their arguments. Science has therefore tended to depress many who, without accepting materialistic opinions, have been affected by the march of thought. On the whole we may say that science has tended to positivism, agnosticism, and in a word to a negative view of things spiritual.

16

The characteristics of the Victorian Age, then, centred about this intellectual battle between the forces of reason and the forces of revelation: between theology with its demands on belief, and the new scientific materialism with its collection of disturbing facts. The temper of the age was violent, as we may see by the reception accorded to Darwin's book. It created a sensation. All the forces of established religion were brought to bear upon it. It was commonly objected that such criticisms of the Bible were a wanton unsettlement of the faith of simple people, and in 1864, five years after the appearance of the *Origin of Species*, the Oxford Declaration on Inspiration and Eternal Punishment was signed by eleven thousand members of the clergy. This was a curious document. According to Archbishop Tait the effect of this declaration was that 'all questions of physical science should be referred to the written words of Holy Scripture'.

Meanwhile, however, archæology went its own way, and among its discoveries we should perhaps record the first example of Paleolithic Cave Art. But we should also hasten to mention that the first studies in anthropology were beginning to occupy the thoughts of scholars about this time. The effect of a book like Frazer's *The Golden Bough*—an inquiry into the origins of religious belief—cannot be over-estimated; and side by side with anthropological speculation came the first attempts to deal with Jesus as a historical figure. The biographical *Jesus* of Renan had caused almost the same storm in Europe as *The Origin of Species* in England.

The narrow iron-bound theology of the Victorian simply could not accommodate all the facts which were piling up in the laboratories of the scientists. It was all very well to appeal to belief. The age, with its materialist bias and its young utilitarian science, thought that reason would be a surer guide in human affairs. 'Scientific proof' became one of the watchwords of the day.

Tennyson's *Ulysses*, you may remember, burned 'to follow knowledge, like a sinking star, beyond the utmost bound of human thought'. It was a desire which found an echo in every Victorian heart, and it was to be gratified in the most literal sense by the scientists of the next century. For the trouble with scientific thought today is that it does appear to have reached something like the boundary-line of human thought—the boundary-line of its conceptual abilities.

There are several other aspects of the Victorian Age which deserve mention. So far I have tried to stick to those which altered the concept of history in time. But while we cannot stay to treat any of these great systems in detail, we should not forget to add to them the name of Marx, written in the margin of our note-books. *Das Kapital* was written in 1867. Though Marxism was the ugly duckling among the philosophies fathered on us by scientific rationalism, yet the evolution of social ideas and reforms is an important part of the Victorian picture, though not absolutely vital to our own research on *Ulysses*. I would prefer to turn to Logical Positivism for a moment as a part of the Victorian inheritance. Auguste Comte, who propounded this philosophy, was born in 1798. He believed that every science followed a clearly defined historical curve, and might be divided up into three stages of belief. In the first, the animistic stage, people believed that the universe was ruled over by the personifications of various deities: Gods, Goddesses, Nymphs, etc. In the second stage these mythical conceptions became depersonified and were replaced by conceptual entities like 'force', 'gravity' and other such mechanical ideas. In the third or positive stage even these mechanical ideas would die out and would be replaced with a purely negative attitude towards phenomena. The idea of natural forces would die out and science would no longer offer us explanations of why things happened: it would simply content itself with keeping a log of happenings and of studying them within a provisional frame of thought.

Now the philosophy of scientific materialism which played so great a part in the Victorian outlook had taken over the full equipment of forces, levers, pulleys and laws, bequeathed to it by Newton.

Ranged against the forces of this mechanistic philosophy we find representatives of many differing camps, both religious and æsthetic. They saw with alarm that the scientist in his arrogance was setting up shop as a theologian. Up till now the mechanical universe postulated by the mechanist had left elbow-room for the Deity. But the materialists of *Ulysses'* age were beginning to question whether God could not be replaced by some hypothetical first cause—some purely chemical force which set the whole business off. Assailed on all fronts by science, geology, archæology, theology fought on doggedly, but without avail. The age was a materialistic age and its God was reason.

*Ulysses* of course ante-dates this period by a decade or two. But you can see from his style that his world has not been threatened as yet, has not been afflicted with doubt and despair. I would like to suggest that a good deal of the despair in *Gerontion* comes of a realization that the world has gone off the rails. Food, as you know, takes time to reach the stomach; and I suggest that Gerontion expresses all the disillusion of the 1890's.

The effect of these ideas upon the Victorian world has been very well expressed by Sherwood Taylor:

> The whole of the literature, art and philosophy of the past was based on the axioms that the changes of the world were a drama enacted on the unchanging scene of nature by un-changing man—a little lower than the angels and immea-surably above the beasts who had no understanding. The art, literature and morality of Europe were based on the Bible, understood in the old simple way. The later Victorians

isolated in vast deserts of space and time, with God seemingly removed to the dim status of a remote Architect of the World, could no longer feel themselves one with those who dwelt contentedly in the little universe of past ages. . . . And so the Victorian moved out of man's ancestral home, with its temples, palaces, cottages and cathedrals, golden with age, tenderly formed by the hands of the masters, into a fine new city of science—so convenient, so hygienic, so reasonably planned—but devoid of human tenderness and ancient beauty. This loss has never been repaired and man to-day is still a displaced person in a land he has yet to make his home.

I could not hope for a clearer summing up of the message we find implicit in Gerontion's attitude. It is a message which afterwards received amplification in *The Waste Land* which has had such a great effect upon the poetic tradition in England. The whole fabric of the poem is shot with reminiscences of history, poetry, myth, all tangled up as they are in *Gerontion*. The central message is, of course, disillusion. Gerontion himself might easily have figured in *The Waste Land*. He is written in the same tone of voice.

> And it is not by any concitation
> Of the backward devils.
> I would meet you upon this honestly.
> I that was near your heart was removed therefrom
> To lose beauty in terror, terror in inquisition.
> I have lost my passion: why should I need to keep it
> Since what is kept must be adulterated?
> I have lost my sight, smell, hearing, taste and touch:
> How should I use them for your closer contact?

But do not think that *Gerontion* is simply and solely a revolt against Victorian materialism. That would be a ridiculous over-simplification. Materialism itself was not a new enemy, though it was most firmly entrenched behind the new discoveries of science. But the general philosophy of materialism was, I suppose, a legacy left to us by Hobbes, which received a new impetus from the discoveries of applied science.

Hobbes believed that the whole world consisted simply of matter and motion, and that the only reality was matter. Man was an animal with a body made of matter while his thoughts and emotions arose from the purely mechanical motions of the atoms with which he was constructed.

It followed from this of course that when the scientist managed to break down matter to its smallest part he would find it something substantial, something solid however small, a piece of matter. This is what the early Victorians believed. But there was a surprise in store for them.

There is only one other aspect of Victorian science which is important to grasp, and that is the relation it assumed to exist between subject and object, observer and observed. In the so-called exact sciences subject and object were taken to be two distinct things: so that a description of any part of the universe was considered a judgment quite independent of the observer—or of any subjective conditions in which he found himself. Science claimed an ABSOLUTE OBJECTIVITY in its judgments about the world.

This view of the subject-object relationship was only discarded in the light of Einstein's Relativity Theory which was born some twenty years later. This is a fact which is vital to our understanding of the age we live in, and the literature which characterizes that age. You will understand me when I say that *Ulysses* is an objective poem and *Gerontion* a subjective one. In *Ulysses* the camera is, so to speak, facing outwards to the world, recording the fears and preoccupations of the hero objectively; *Gerontion* is exactly the opposite. The camera, if I may repeat the metaphor, is focused inwards upon the secret hopes and fears of the old hero. It is a moving picture of the processes of the unconscious at work. In Tennyson's poem we deduce the inner state of the hero from his statements about things outside himself. Eliot's poem demands something more. It is a detective story in little and we must all the time be watching for clues and hints if we are to understand what is going on.

The subject-object relationship is one that is worth some thought. If we mark off the 100 years which separate us from the writers whose work betrays a Semantic Disturbance—I am thinking of Rimbaud, Laforgue, Lewis Carroll, Nietzsche and others of the same *genre*—we see, I think, a gradually increasing curve of subjectivity, through, let us say, Dickens, Tolstoy, Dostoievski, Proust, Joyce. The vision of the artist seems to be gradually turning inwards upon himself. Perhaps we can see this state of affairs in the general cosmology of the age also, if we follow out the curve of knowledge, through Victorian materialism, agnosticism, and classical objectivity until we reach the present day. Of course we cannot hope to dismantle and examine in detail the great systems of ideas which we shall encounter on such a journey. Our object is to try and illuminate literature from a new angle; so you will not complain, I hope, if I take from each system only the ideas which have some direct bearing upon the problem we have set ourselves—which is to discover how Ulysses became Gerontion.

Of course no picture of this kind could possibly claim completeness for itself unless it dealt fairly thoroughly with such diverse thinkers as Spencer and Bradley, with theologians like Manning, and with philosophers like James and Bagehot and Ruskin. But any attempt of this kind would lead us too far from the main path of our study. I propose to show you the sources of the insecurity which beset the Victorians and which was later to reflect itself in the poetry of the first half of the twentieth century. It would be just as important to show you how the mechanical universe as an idea was overturned by the work of the physicists, and how our whole conception of ourselves as egos was altered by the findings of psychology.

But all this will have one object. To give you, if possible, an account of how our ideas about Time changed, and of how our ideas about the ego were first formed. Time as history and evolution took its first blow from Darwin, from geology and archæology. Time as an idea took its second great blow from Einstein. The one thing which differentiated the new physics—the physics of today, that is—from the old (Einstein's from Newton's) is the idea of the nature of space and time and their relationship. Under the new theory space was conceived of as being *n*-dimensional, with time as the fourth of its dimensions. This completely revolutionized our whole attitude to the universe, and if we are to understand the time-literature of Joyce and Virginia Woolf no less than the poetry of *The Waste Land*, we must strike up a nodding acquaintance with the new theory. Similarly if we are to understand the new egocentric growth of art we should know a little about Freud. If time is, as I believe, the measure of our death-consciousness, you cannot revise your concept of it without affecting our ideas of death and life. Some of these ideas are germinating among the oracular utterances of *Gerontion*; others are to be found in the *Four Quartets* of Eliot and in the *Duinese Elegies* of Rilke no less than in Joyce's *Ulysses*. Time is one of the great clues to the modern outlook.

CHAPTER 2

## SPACE TIME AND POETRY

With the twentieth century,- Physics, like the other
sciences, advanced into uncertainties. In the face of relativity, the quantum theory, and the electron, we were once
more moving in 'worlds not realized'. If God were a mathematician, mathematicians should bring us back to God. . . .
We saw that modern man is tempted, almost compelled,
to regulate this idea (Time) by the face of a clock and the
pages of a calendar. This system is indispensable to an age of
fixed hours and appointments, but cannot ever satisfy man's
consciousness of what passes in his own head. It suggests or
confirms the fiction that life is a sequence of continuous yet
distinct moments, a perpetual birth of instantaneous impressions, whereas all artistic and imaginative experience insists
that life as we perceive it is duration. For example the first
note of fugue is still present when the last note is struck; the
first scene in a well-constructed drama is as close to us as the
episode on which the curtain descends. All life is fusion as
well as flux . . . and Past combines with Present to form the
outline of the Future. Some visionaries claim the power to
relive their own antecedents and to be present at what is
going to happen. These persuasions might be, and generally
are, dismissed as wishful thinking, though the acceptance of
eternity implies the acceptance that all facts are forever present; but now science was beginning to hint that Time takes
place within us. . . . Thus the modern spirit of inquiry is
leading us back towards ancient Oriental mysticism and
medieval theology. . . .

H. V. ROUTH
*English Literature and Ideas in the Twentieth Century*

WE have not far to go with the history of Joyce's *Ulysses*
thought before we come to some new scientific ideas which
have a direct bearing upon time, and which, I make bold
to say, can be seen reflected in the new style of writing

24

for which our age has become distinguished. To the materialists, you remember, subject and object were divided off from one another, while matter—however far you broke it down—would conform to the ideas of mass developed out of Newton's mechanics. Matter, they thought, would presumably have a solid core which, however infinitesimal, could be measured and weighed and studied. As soon as the laws governing its structure were understood we should have the whole riddle of the universe in our hands.

Science, as you know, is the art of imaginative arrangement, and its raw material is fact deduced from experiment. Soon the stage was crowded with so-called facts which could not be accommodated into the old way of thinking—the mechanical theory of the universe.

Electricity and the discovery of the first radio-active substances in 1898 raised these problems in the minds of the scientists, and they went to work to try and solve them. First we should mention an investigation into the properties of radiation published by Planck in 1899. He set out to discover why the energy given off by radio-active substances did not transform those bodies wholly into radiation. In order to frame his ideas satisfactorily he was forced to wonder whether he should not give up two philosophic ideas which, up to then, had been regarded as absolutely fundamental to any understanding of the universe. One was time, as we visualized it, and the other was causality. This, you will agree, is simply hair-raising. In 1903 Rutherford and Soddy tried to postulate the fundamental laws of radio-activity and arrived at a very astonishing conclusion which seemed to suggest that the ultimate laws of nature were simply not causal at all. It remained for Einstein to join up these two discoveries with his theory of Relativity, under the terms of which we were presented with a new kind of space and time.

By this time you will perhaps be imagining that I have

gone rather far off the track of our enquiry. After all, you might ask, what on earth can the relativity theory have to do with T. S. Eliot's style? I am not suggesting that modern poetry is constructed to illustrate the quantum theory, but I do suggest that it unconsciously reproduces something like the space-time continuum in the way that it uses words and phrases: and the way in which its forms are cyclic rather than extended. Time, both in the novel and in the poem, has taken on a different aspect. Think of a novel by Scott, let us say, and see whether when you open it you are not given an account of the characters in terms of historic process. The hero is born, he grows up, acts and dies—or marries. Before Joyce the novel was constructed, so to speak, lengthways, as was the average poem. The new consciousness of the century with its emphasis on time produced other criteria. The naturalistic school, as André Gide points out in his *Les Faux Monnayeurs*, spoke about a slice of life. 'The mistake,' he adds, through one of his characters, 'the mistake that school made was always to cut its slice in the same direction, always lengthwise, in the direction of time. Why not cut it up and down? Or across? As for me, I don't want to cut it at all. You see what I mean. I want to put everything into my novel and not snip off my material either here or there.' That would stand as a very good working credo for the stream-of-consciousness novel.

What of the new idea of time, and the new attitude to matter? Let us touch only the fringes of the subject. As we saw, the scientific materialist was shut off from the world by his egocentric view of things. It is important to realize that Einstein's theory joined up subject and object, in very much the same way as it joined up space and time. Now what is important to us here are not the equations—even if we understand them—but the symbolic act of joining what is separated.

Now in the mechanical view of things which our great-grandfathers inherited from Newton the conceptions of 'matter' 'space' and 'time' had absolute validity. But when the physicist began to break matter down into its parts, and found that sometimes it behaved like a wave and sometimes like a particle, it became rapidly obvious that some new conception was needed if we were ever going to make a coherent picture of the universe without neglecting any of these puzzling facts.

While this was going on the astronomers had been amassing quantities of new material about the behaviour of stars. This had to be fitted in as well. How? The world of science is like a nursery crowded with different toys. The scientist, sitting on the floor, tries to find some system which would satisfactorily explain their function. Finally he decides upon a function common to them all—they are for play. But it is extremely doubtful whether from such a collection of toys he will ever be able to deduce the existence of the child who collected them. The materialists thought one could. The modern scientist has so far lost confidence in his powers that he has given up trying. He is content with a provisional view instead of an absolute one.

It had been known, for example, that a body, a piece of matter, behaved as if it acquired greater mass when it was charged with electricity. Purely as a matter of interest it was decided to determine how much of the mass of an electron was its own, and how much was due to its electric charge. The measurement was made with the truly astounding result that the whole mass of the electron was found to be due to its electric charge. So that the electron was not a piece of 'ordinary matter' at all. It was simply an electric charge. You can see how astonishing this experiment must have been. It was the first indication to come from science that the material universe was not the solid, substantial, objective thing people had taken it to be. What was it? 'To talk,' says a scientific writer, 'of an electric charge existing apart from ordinary matter seemed

27

to many minds as incomprehensible as talking about motion without anything that moves. Indeed the discovery could not be understood until our notions of matter became more abstract. The notion of substance had to be replaced by the notion of behaviour.

The solid pragmatic universe, then, melted between our fingers. Matter became a phantom. Now in order to obtain a coherent view of the bewildering world of science Einstein formulated a theory which everybody has heard about and very few people understand. As far as we are concerned only two aspects of it interest us: its attitude to time, and its attitude to the subject-object relationship. The materialists, as we saw, assumed that the divorce was complete—that the observer could observe the object and surprise it in its pure state. The theory of relativity contradicted that view. It showed us that the picture which each observer makes of the world is in some degree subjective. Even if different observers all take their pictures at the same moment of time, and from the same point in space, these pictures will not be alike—unless the observers happen to be moving at the same speed. Only then would they be identical.

Einstein, in order to give his new theory a shape, suddenly saw that the space and time ideas we were using were not flexible enough to fit the picture. He suggested a marriage of the two into a four-dimensional volume which he called a 'continuum'. Time, then, was given a new role to play—it was not the old extended time of the materialists but a new time-space hybrid. Time and space, fixed together in this manner, gave one a completely new idea of what reality might be. The materialist thought that an object to have existence must take advantage of three dimensions of space: time was added to this picture—very much as the sound-track was added to the cinema, and was made to synchronize with the movement of the actor's lips. But Einstein's time was not a past-present-future ob-

ject of this kind. It was a sort of time which contained all
time in every moment of time. A difficult idea to grasp no
doubt. In that popular book on science called *The*
*Mysterious Universe* by the late Sir James Jeans the following explanation of the new time is given:

> It may be that time, from its beginning to the end of
> eternity, is spread before us in the picture, but we are in con-
> tact with only one instant, just as a bicycle-wheel is in con-
> tact with only one point of the road. . . . As Plato expressed
> it twenty-three centuries earlier in the *Timaeus*: 'The past
> and future are created species of time which we uncon-
> sciously but wrongly transfer to the eternal essence. We say
> *was, is, will be,* but the truth is that *is* alone can properly be
> used'.

In the space-time continuum, then, time is an 'Is-ness'—
a concept which was unknown to the age of Ulysses—
except perhaps as always by intuition to certain poets and
mystics.

Another aspect of the Relativity theory is the manner in
which it sidetracks causality. Our belief in causality is a
very strongly grounded one. We live by it. It has for
generations been regarded as the bedrock of philosophy.
Until today only the mystic or the saint has dared to
disown it as part of the behaviour of matter, which he
claims is 'illusion'. But is it possible to think in other terms
than those dictated by a belief in causality? If I plant a
seed a tree will grow and not a man. *Why not a man?* Because . . . you know as well as I do. Yet the new theory of
the physicists invites us to modify this conception if not
actually to question its validity. So far as phenomena are
concerned, we are told, the uniformity of nature dis-
appears. The Principle of Indeterminacy, as it is called,
is founded upon the theory that we cannot observe the
course of nature without disturbing it. This is the complete opposite of the strict determinism which has reigned

in science up to now: and this is one of the great revolutions in thought which characterize the age we are thinking about.

If reality is somehow extra-causal, then a whole new vista of ideas is opened up—a territory hitherto only colonized by intuition. If the result of every experiment, of every motion of nature, is completely unforeseen and unpredictable—then everything is perpetually brand new, everything is, if you care to think of it like that, a miracle.

Under the terms of the new idea a precise knowledge of the outer world becomes an impossibility. This is because we and the outer world (subject and object) constitute a whole. If we are part of a unity we can no longer objectivize it successfully. 'If we still wish to think of the happenings in the phenomenal world as governed by causal law we must suppose that these happenings are determined in some substratum of the world which lies beyond the world of phenomena, and also beyond our access.' I quote from Sir James Jeans' *Physics and Philosophy*. And later in the same book, in discussing the new time, he says: 'It seems at least conceivable that what is true of perceived objects may also be true of perceiving minds; just as there are wave-pictures for light and electricity, so there may be a corresponding picture for consciousness. When we view ourselves in space and time our consciousnesses are obviously the separate individuals of a particle-picture, when we pass beyond space and time (presumably into the continuum which is formed of a mixture of both) they may perhaps form ingredients of a single continuous stream of life. As it is with light and electricity, so it may be with life; the phenomena may be individuals carrying on separate existences in space and time, while in the deeper reality beyond space and time we may all be members of one body. In brief, modern physics is not altogether antagonistic to an objective idealism like that of Hegel.'

Now while the conceptual ability of the scientist seems

to have become landlocked within the frame of his 'continuum', the material accumulation of knowledge is still increasing. We are finding more and more ways of applying scientific knowledge, yet our knowledge of what reality or the universe *is* has not increased. Time has become a thick opaque medium, welded to space—no longer the quickly flowing river of the Christian hymns, moving from here to there along a marked series of stages. But an always-present yet always recurring thing. You will begin to see that to think according to the terms of relativity one has to train the mind to do something rather extraordinary: to accept two contradictory ideas as simultaneously true.

I do not think it is stretching a point too far to say that the work of Joyce and Proust, the poetry of Eliot and Rilke, is an attempt to present the material of human and supernatural affairs in the form of poetic continuum, where the language no less than the objects observed are impregnated with the new time. In Dickens, in Dostoievski you are aware of a natural progress of the plot from one point to another along a defined and charted scale. In Proust and Joyce you see something like a slow-motion camera at work. Their books do not proceed along a straight line, but in a circular manner, coiling and uncoiling upon themselves, embedded in the stagnant flux and reflux of a medium which is always changing yet always the same. This attitude towards the material of the work has its effect on character also. Characters have a significance almost independent of the actions they engage in: they hang above the time-track which leads from birth to action, and from action to death: and, spreading out time in this manner, contribute a significance to everything about them. An article of clothing worn by a character becomes as significant as anything he does, or any drama he enacts. If there is any movement at all it is circular, cyclic, and significant only because it is repeated. Proust took the lifetime of a society as his subject, yet despite the vast canvas his book is almost a still life. Joyce in *Ulysses* restricted himself to the events of a single day, magnified upon the screen of the new time-idea. Fully aware that in treating time like this he might lay himself open to form-lessness in his art, Joyce took the wise precaution of model-ling his book upon *The Odyssey*. The relationship is a very artificial one, and if *Ulysses* has form in the ordinary sense we must thank Homer for it. That it has significance, how-ever, nobody can deny. When we come to discuss Freud we shall, I hope, be able to discuss this aspect of the book more fully.

The physicist deplores any attempt to deal with space-time in metaphors. Relativity, he claims, is a purely mathematical theory and can only be understood by mathematicians. In spite of this several eminent men of science have made an attempt to describe the theory of Relativity in non-technical terms. None of these attempts has been very successful in my opinion. There has even been an attempt, by Alexander, to construct a religious frame around the idea of space-time. His attempt to link up space-time with Deity is interesting because it shows the way the wind is blowing. At some point the cosmologist must pronounce upon the real world, for the benefit of the people living in it who want to understand it better, and who want to learn how to live in it more successfully. It is useless doing what the physicist has done—which is to leave us all embedded, so to speak, in Euclidean space and time, while his own imagination is busy with the new realm. I do not see why lack of mathematical ability should prevent us from discovering what he is thinking.

Alexander, in his book called *Space, Time and Deity*, sug-gests that the space-time material is the primordial reality out of which things have evolved. He claims that every-thing in the world was made of space-time stuff, so to speak, and that by gradual differentiation of matter life

32

arose, which is developing slowly into consciousness, and so into Deity. Everyone had been in the habit of regarding space-time as a creation of the human mind. Alexander reversed this idea and declared that mind was only a function of the space-time stuff in its gradual evolution towards Deity.

In the literature of the last decade there has been a distinct growth of interest in mysticism, and more noticeably in Eastern religion. The first religious classics of the Indians and Chinese were translated about the turn of the century. The Theosophical Society was founded in 1903. The early thought of Yeats and A. E. among others was much coloured by theosophical speculation. Interest in these matters died away and has only recently appeared in the wake of Rilke, Eliot and Valéry—to name three poets who are distinguished by a mystical outlook. It is worth pointing out that these Eastern religions, whether Indian or Chinese, offer us one or two ideas which are not completely incompatible with some of the propositions of relativity. They claim to side-track causality. The escape from the cycle of birth and rebirth into 'Nirvana' promises a new timeless condition which is not subject to intellectual or linguistic qualification. Reality, they tell us, is illusion or appearance.

I mention these facts for what they are worth. It is possible that science and religion may yet find a common ground in some conception capable of uniting the two. Already a brilliant development along these lines has been achieved in the almost unknown books of Francis J. Mott.* He has immeasurably extended the boundaries of Freud's ideas upon the ego, and at the same time provided for a happy marriage between reason and illumination without sacrificing the claims of either. His work, *The Grand Design of the Oedipus Complex*, sets forth these ideas which will be of interest to all poets and students alike. It is a book as characteristic of the new age as Freud's *Interpreta-*

*tion of Dreams* was to the preceding one, and despite its limitations it is not less important in my opinion.

At the moment, however, we are still busy trying to prove that relativity squares with the known facts about the universe—which is our own way of getting æsthetic pleasure out of ideas. Einstein himself, in an interview given to the American press, recently said:

> I maintain that the cosmic religious feeling is the strongest and noblest incitement to scientific research. You will hardly find one among the profounder sort of scientific minds without a peculiar religious feeling of his own. The individual feels the nothingness of human desires and aims, and the sublimity and marvellous order which reveal themselves both in nature and in the world of thought. He looks on individual existence as a sort of prison and wants to experience the universe as a single significant whole.

This, you will agree, is a far cry from the cocksure attitude of the Victorian materialist. In place of the pragmatically and eternally true, science has placed a new, a more humble objective: provisional truth, as complete as possible, and as fully aware of the limitations of thought as possible.

But what of the new space-time idea? We find ourselves up against the barrier of mathematics. Unless we understand the equations, they tell us, we will never understand the relativity principle. Here I would like to turn for help to a Renaissance philosopher called Giordano Bruno. He was a contemporary of Shakespeare. He resembles Einstein in one thing—he threw Aristotle overboard. Now while Bruno had no mathematical apparatus to frame his ideas for him, no curved geometries, he did have a distinct and unique idea of the universe which at some points resembles the space-time conception. He found himself very much in the position in which we students are today. He had to depend on images and metaphors to express his view of the universe. For him the space and time which Aristotle had regarded as finite in duration and extent though infinitely divisible—took on other proportions. They were unlimited in their dimensions yet consisted of discrete minimal parts. Here is Bruno's description of time:

> In every point of duration is beginning without end and end without beginning. It is the centre of two infinities. Therefore the whole of duration is one infinite instant, both beginning and end, as immeasurable space is an infinite minimum or centre.'

In another place he adds:

> God does all things without deliberation, anxiety, or perplexity—provides for innumerable species and for an infinite number of individuals, not in any order of succession but at once and all together. He is not like a finite agent, doing things one by one, with many acts—an infinite number of acts for an infinite number of things—but he does everything, past, present and future, with one simple and unique act.

Now I have quoted Bruno for two reasons: firstly because being forced to think in terms of analogy and metaphor he is better able to give us a picture of the simultaneity, so to speak, of time, than a mathematician would be: secondly we know how much Joyce was influenced by the ideas of Bruno at the time when he was composing *Finnegan's Wake*. I dare not claim that his system squares with relativity at all points. I do not know enough about it to suggest that. But there are several resemblances which are striking. In discussing the monad, for example, he says:

> Nothing variable or composite consists at two moments of time wholly of the same parts and the same order of parts; since the efflux and influx of atoms is continuous, and therefore not even from the primary integrating parts will you be able to name a thing as the same twice.

35

We have seen how time as history received its death-blow from geology and from Darwin; now we see that time as process, as extension along a series of points, has been halted, has been, so to speak, dammed up. Now language, as I have tried to show, is very dependent upon our conception of time. I would like to suggest that the growth of these new ideas has had a disruptive effect upon linguistic structure. The relation of subject verb and object in the simple sentence has been disturbed, no less than the relation of the sentence to the paragraph and the paragraph to the book. Before this new idea grew up language was so to speak Aristotelian in structure: now it is trying to render a sort of immediacy of impact—the impact of all time crowded into one moment of time. I can do no better than to quote Rilke in this context. In one of his notes upon poetry he delivered himself of his views upon the nature of time in the following words:

> We, of this earth and this to-day, are not for a moment hedged in by the world of time, nor bound within it: we are incessantly flowing over and over to those who preceded us and those who apparently come after us. In that widest 'open' world, all *are*—one cannot say 'simultaneously', for the very falling away of time conditions their existing. . . .
>
> (*Letters*, 1925).

I have already described time as the measure of our death-consciousness, and suggested that if you change our ideas about time you cannot but help change our ideas of death also. It is one of the paradoxes of the new space-time that, if time is really spread out in this way, *we can just as easily situate death in the present as in the future*. It is this multiple state birth-life-death in one which the poet is trying to capture. But since the linguistic equipment he has taken over is inadequate to the task he is forced to refashion it, to transform it into a weapon capable of rendering immediacy. In 1923 Rilke wrote:

It lies in the nature of these poems, in their condensation and abbreviation (in the way they often state lyric totals instead of lining up the stages necessary to the result) that they seem intended to be grasped, rather through inspiration in those similarly directed than with what is called 'understanding'.

The phrase 'lyric totals' should give us a clue to the oracular utterances of Gerontion and to the apparent lack of grammatical continuity between the various parts of the poem. It is a faithful enough reflection of a new cosmological attitude, and it faithfully performs what it sets out to do—to state a 'lyric total'. We should also notice that in form it is cyclic—it ends where it began. This 'cyclic' feature is one which becomes more and more apparent in the art of the age. In his later poems, where faith and affirmation replace the sterility and exhaustion of Gerontion's attitude, T. S. Eliot makes a far more faithful picture of this new territory. One of the *Four Quartets* is built upon the phrase 'In my end is my beginning', and this is repeated in the form of fugue, sometimes changed, sometimes turned upside down, and sometimes repeated. It is in small things like this that we discern the new values of the age. Nothing has permanent value—that is really the message behind it—everything depends upon its context in a given system, depends on the way you use it. The identity of opposites precludes any complete and final judgment upon reality.

The marriage of subject and object is something which I would prefer to leave until we come to study the influence of Freud. Let us return to the question of death-situated-in-the-present—if the idea does not seem to you completely fantastic. In this connection I would like to return to Rilke. Speaking of the *Duinese Elegies* he says:

Affirmation of life and death appears as one in *The Elegies*. To admit one without the other is, as is here learned and celebrated, a limitation that in the end excludes all infinity. Death is the *side of life* that is turned away from us: we must try to achieve the fullest consciousness of our existence, which is the same in the *two unseparated realms*, inexhaustibly nourished by both. There is neither a here nor a beyond but *the great unity*, in which those creatures who surpass us, the angels, are at home.

This is not only good mysticism, it is a not entirely inadequate view of the kind of thing the relativity philosophers are talking about. Both in the state of language, and in the preoccupation of the contemporary poet, you may see reflections of it.

> Time present and time past
> Are both perhaps present in time future,
> And time future contained in time past.
> If all time is eternally present
> All time is unredeemable.

You probably recognize the quotation. It is from T. S. Eliot's *Burnt Norton*, and I think in the light of what we know about physics we can see—those of us who have not the sensibility or experience to understand straight off— the sort of thing the poet is getting after, the sort of time he is trying to convey. It is a very different idea from that of Victorian 'eternity', this new space-time. It gives a different colour to reality.

In presenting these various facts about the last hundred years of man's thinking and feeling I do not wish to suggest that any one discovery is responsible for any of the others. History is too tightly woven for us to proceed in this manner. Some of these so-called 'new ideas' are thousands of years old. If I suggest that the influence of Freud and Einstein is discernible in the intricate and beautiful workmanship of the modern poet I do not want you to regard it as purely a cause-and-effect study of literature. If you do, then I shall be forced to point out that many of Freud's ideas were anticipated by Nietzsche and Dostoievski, and that some of Einstein's equipment is as old as Pythagoras.

The trouble about thinking and talking is that we must cast our thoughts and our words within the frame of a method. In listening to me you must adopt some of the humility of the modern scientist for whom there are no more 'facts' but simply 'point-events' strung out in reality. The relations we see, or think we see, between ideas, are only useful if we use them as spring-boards from which to jump into reality ourselves. Art describes the kind of reality which is already dead for the artist. Once you fully understand a work of art you no longer have any need of it. So that if we talk about the last hundred years as a progression of a sort, it is simply to suit our arbitrary mode of thought. In reality we are simply making a rough-and-ready star-map of a universe which we do not perfectly understand.

Since we have adopted the historical method there is another curiosity which deserves notice. That is what we might call the 'The Semantic Disturbance'—the disturbance of meaning within the structure of language. I am thinking now of that group of writers Rimbaud, Laforgue, Lewis Carroll, Nietzsche—you will observe that I am putting them all together, regardless of their relative size—which began to struggle with a new kind of problem. In reading them you feel always that the reality they tried to express was beyond the bounds of the linguistic and conceptual apparatus at their command. They worked language so hard that it fell to pieces. They worked so hard to conceive, to grasp and express, this new reality that many of them paid the penalty which lies in wait for those who overwork their sensibility. The fate of Nietzsche, of Van Gogh reminds us of this only too forcibly. Rimbaud frightened himself with his attempt on the absolute which, he felt, lay behind 'un long, immense et raisonné dérèglement de tous les sens'. Their work is characterized by a hysterical subjectivity which nothing, after the turn of the century, can match. How tame, beside Rimbaud and

Laforgue, seem the efforts of the Surréalists. You feel the difference of *timbre* at once, when you pick up Bréton. For where the surrealists are trying to provoke an emotion Rimbaud was trying to *describe a state*. What was this state? We cannot say clearly. But we feel it every time we hear those agonized accents which reach us in the latest work of Nietzsche, in Rimbaud, and even behind the padded contentment of Lewis Carroll.

I would like to suggest that the new reality, which disrupted language and lives wholesale, was grasped, conceived and assimilated about the turn of the century. After 1900 the artist seems to regain authority over his medium without having to pay the price of madness. Perhaps I am wrong. It is tempting however to suggest that the discoveries of Freud and Einstein helped him, by their firm conceptual treatment of the unknown, and by the uncompromising honesty with which they dealt with the two universes—the universe outside man, and the universe inside. The artist, you feel, has no right any more to cast himself bodily into the breach, to sacrifice his reason in order to grasp reality. An artist who goes mad today is not doing his job properly. Yet when you think of that great constellation of madmen which lit up the artistic heavens in mid-Victorian times you cannot but admire their heroism and self-dedication. Here is Laforgue, in the character of *Hamlet:*

Oui, ce qui manque à Hamlet c'est la liberté. Je ne demande rien à personne, moi. Je suis sans ami; je n'ai pas un ami qui pourrait raconter mon histoire, un ami qui me précéderait partout pour m'éviter les explications qui me tuent. Je n'ai pas une jeune fille qui saurait me goûter. Ah oui, une garde-malade. Une garde-malade pour l'amour de l'art, ne donnant ses baisers qu'à des mourants, des gens in-extrémis, qui ne pourraient par conséquent s'en vanter ensuite. Et au fond, dire que j'existe. Que j'ai ma vie à moi. L'éternité en soi avant ma naissance, l'éternité en soi après ma mort. Et passer ainsi mes jours à tuer le temps.

*what ( I can't read French — that's it.*

What are we to say in the face of this anguish of spirit which so far surpasses the linguistic and conceptual ability of the artist that he is forced to express himself in a series of groans and exclamations?

> Et qu'on me regardait passer dans les rues en s'étonnant de mon allure triste? Et que d'aucuns se tueraient devant l'énigme de ma vie. O Kate, si tu savais. Ce drame-ci, ce n'est rien, je l'ai conçu et travaillé au milieu de répugnantes préoccupations domestiques.

If I quote Laforgue it is because Eliot has already confessd that this French poet was an early influence. Some of the dislocation of language, some of the anguish of Laforgue, together with his ability to take legendary *personae* and write poetical autobiography round them, we shall be able to trace in the verse of Eliot's middle period. But his latest poetic development in the long poem called *Four Quartets* is far more representative of the age's preoccupations than *Gerontion* is. This long poem belongs beside Rilke's *Duinese Elegies* as a masterly excursion into a new realm of sensibility.

For our purpose, however, the comparison between Tennyson's *Ulysses* and *Gerontion* is necessary until we understand a few more of the ideas which separate them, which decree their different modes of expression. Here again I am anxious not to suggest that our historical view is anything but arbitrary. We have taken a period in order to try and distinguish some of its major characteristics. It would be impertinent to bind it too closely by the terms of reference which we seek to impose upon it. I am reminded as I talk that both the ravings of Blake and the meditations of Kierkegaard stand outside the borders of this period. But if we take a thesis and try to force history or reality to conform to it we will only be violating our own intentions in setting out such a scheme of study. We wish to understand contemporary literature better. We do not expect to

reach either a final understanding of it, or a final judgment upon the age which produced it. Our contribution is
a provisional one.

We have spoken of the Semantic Disturbance. There is
another characteristic of the period under review which
is interesting to observe. That is the gradual interest that
literature begins to take in double-personality. From the
time of Balzac's *Seraphita* we observe a gradually growing
interest in the theme of the double which runs side by side
with the gradual curve of subjectivity, through Dostoievski
(*The Double*), Edgar Allen Poe, Stevenson (*Dr. Jekyll and
Mr. Hyde*) up to Oscar Wilde (*The Picture of Dorian Gray*).
Of course the double is not a novelty. Shakespeare used
the idea more than once to produce situations the key to
which lay in mistaken identity. Psychologists suggest that
here perhaps we have the clue to repressed or unconscious
homosexuality in his nature. This may be so. But there is
one curious thing about the theme of the double in the
period we are examining. In nearly every case we are
given a double which is either a saint, a criminal or a
monster. Stevenson, as you probably know, dreamed the
story of Dr. Jekyll and Mr. Hyde. His wife was awakened
by his shouts and exclamations. She in turn woke him up
and he told her that he had been dreaming up a fine 'bogy-
man story', which he immediately proceeded to write,
there and then.

In this same context I am reminded of a phrase of Rimbaud's which might almost stand as an epigraph to any
book about this period. 'Je est un autre.' It is a magical
phrase, for it not only expresses this feeling of *dédoublement*
but in its very dislocation of the grammatical form it pre-
figures much that is to come. It is both mantic and semantic in its implications. If we are to take this preoccupation
as significant—and there are many other examples of it in
the literature of the period under review—we might
imagine that it signified a deep-seated split in the psyche

which, after the turn of the century, was no longer possible
or necessary. Here again, would it be unjust to attribute
much of the joining and reconciling influence to the discoveries made by Freud about the unconscious impulses?
It is something which each of us must decide for himself.
It would perhaps be possible to say, however, that part of
this split, this duality in the psyche, might be seen reflected
in the general philosophic view of subject divorced from
object, which is one of the beliefs that haunted *Ulysses'* age.
In the poets of the Semantic Disturbance you see an
attempt being made to join up subject and object, to
marry the reality around them and renounce their individual isolation. They were very far from the contemporary
view which, once again, I would like to try and express in
the words of Giordano Bruno:

> How can immobility, subsistence, entity, truth, be under-
> stood by that which is always different from itself, always
> acting and becoming in different ways? What truth, what
> representation can be depicted or impressed when the pupils
> of the eyes are dispersed into water, the water into vapour,
> the vapour into flame, the flame into air. . . . ? Into the very
> life of the generous soul there enter, accordingly, the con-
> trarieties by which, on a lower plane, the soul is governed
> . . . There is no pleasure of generation on the one side with-
> out pain of corruption on the other; and the things that are
> becoming with those that are decaying are conjoined in one
> and the same composite being. . . .

It is a refusal to accept the terms of the duality under
which we live that characterizes those artists of whom we
have spoken. Slowly, painfully, the lesson was learned—
but even today can it be said that it has been thoroughly
learned?

*Gerontion* imitates many of the features of the age of
Rimbaud and Dostoievski. *The Waste Land* continues the
attack; but the target seems to be no longer what it was for
Rimbaud—nothing less than the absolute. By the time the

end of the century was reached poets were still carrying on
the linguistic experiments bequeathed to them by the
semantic innovators. But their terms of reference had been
narrowed by a new humility. Like the scientist they were
no longer concerned with explaining reality, but with
teaching us how to accommodate ourselves to it. The
curve from 1920-1940, though it follows out the general
structural pattern which we have laid down for it, is
quickened by a new attitude. But this we will deal with
later.

So far I have avoided the purely sociological interest in
the writing of our contemporaries because it seemed the
most obvious part of poetry today. You do not have to go
very far to discover withering criticisms of the utilitarian
world which we have built up around us—a world so
destructive of human and spiritual values. If you choose
to discuss *Gerontion* in these terms you would not be wrong,
for the poem is also a jeremiad against the condition in
which humanity finds itself today. I do not need, I think,
to mention either the last war or the latest—or even the
war to come—as another possible determinant of poetic
style. That aspect of art has been done—perhaps we might
say overdone. I prefer to stick to a very general pattern, in
the hope that you can fill in the detail to suit your own
temperamental inclinations.

The only place where I would like to lay some stress is
in claiming that art is only a dialect of a language, and
that we get a wider view of it if we don't rope it off from
everything else and try and consider it as an isolated
phenomenon. There are, as you probably know, many
kinds of truth, some of which have little enough to do with
reason as we understand it. Yet all methods of approaching truth are legitimate. They are when all is said and
done only ladders, some long, some short. We must, however, have the courage to discard those ladders which
prove, when we try them, too short to reach our objective.

Mathematics, biology, painting and poetry are different ways of looking at reality and trying to construct æsthetically satisfying pictures of it. The important thing about all these pictures is not their relative truth, but the joy they can communicate. And our feeling for literature can only gain from an appreciation of the fact.

All that I have said about the time-space idea so far I have attempted to illustrate in terms of literature, but my thesis could equally well be illustrated in terms of painting. For example the difference between a strict representational painting and an abstract with the same title is easily enough understood in the light of the subject-object relationship and the changes we have remarked. In the one case the artist has painted the object, and in the other he has painted his feeling about the object instead of the object itself. It is very much the same with the subjectivity of literature today.

In Joyce's *Ulysses*, for example, the indications of space, time, location and so on are hardly given. In some cases one has to infer them. This method would have horrified and puzzled Stendhal or Balzac. But what interests James Joyce is, so to speak, the temporal cocoon that surrounds an object or a character. It is merely a springboard from which he jumps to the network of symbolic associations surrounding it. That is why everything in *Ulysses* is coated in a thick fur of association. If you keep stopping to ask yourself, 'Where is he now?' and: 'What is he doing?' you will be lost. The first article of faith with subjective writing is complete surrender to the associative flux and reflux about the observed object. Virginia Woolf has expressed this attitude very clearly in a passage from her *Common Reader*:

Examine for a moment an ordinary mind on an ordinary day. The mind receives a myriad impressions—trivial, fantastic, evanescent, or engraved with the sharpness of steel.

45

From all sides they come, an incessant shower of innumerable atoms; and as they fall they shape themselves into the life of Monday or Tuesday. . . . So that if a writer were a free man and not a slave, if he could base his work on his own feeling and not upon convention, there would be no plot, no comedy, no tragedy, no love interest, no catastrophe in the accepted style. Life is not a series of gig-lamps symmetrically arranged. Life is a luminous halo, a semi-transparent envelope surrounding us from the beginning of consciousness to the end. Is it not the task of the novelist to convey this varying, this unknown and uncircumscribed spirit?

At any rate, that is the task that both Joyce and Virginia Woolf set themselves. A similar kind of objective lies behind the oracular mumblings of Gerontion, though we cannot know how much the author himself was conscious of the fact.

I spoke a few moments ago about two contradictory ideas being simultaneously true under the terms of the new thought. It is a subject which deserves to be examined. It was foreign to materialist thinking, though of course the theory of the identity of opposites is as old as thought itself. Perhaps it found its way into the scientific framework *via* Hegel, the philosopher. At all events, one distinguishing feature between the new thought and the old is the degree to which it accepts the duality inherent in statement. The Victorians were content with a moralistic, one-way view. The characteristic of our age is the acceptance of duality, and a non-moral view of things.

Let me try and make this clearer. When we judge the blackness or goodness of something we are really measuring it against its opposite. If you say something is 'good' you are really using a graduated yardstick of 'evil' to measure it by. Thus the use of a phrase calls up its opposite —for if we had no idea of evil we should be unable to measure goodness—for we measure one against the other. When we say 'good' we at once introduce the category 'evil', and the same with all the other opposites. But

46

language, you will protest, is built upon what seems to be a dualistic foundation. That is the problem. If the opposites are identical then statement is a relative affair, not, as our great-grandfathers thought, an absolute affair.

Philosophic ideas cut down to different levels in the consciousness of the body politic. Sometimes they are formulated and lie forgotten. At others they penetrate more deeply and influence the generality of people. This question of the inherent duality in things, and an acceptance of it as part of the human limitation, you will find both in the relativity-view and later when you come upon the term 'ambivalence' in Freud. It was perhaps the refusal to accept—or perhaps the impossibility of understanding—this dual principle at the root of thinking and being, that prevented the writers of the Semantic Disturbance from achieving the balance and harmony which their descendants are attempting to formulate and express in their work and presumably in their lives, since the work is a reflection of the life. It is a harmony, a training, which all the really great artists appear to have achieved in their maturity. But it is something for an artist to feel today that he is moving with the tide instead of against it.

If, then, the opposites are really identical from one point of view, they are perhaps reflections of some third unspecified thing? It is a question I wish deliberately to leave hanging in air—indeed I must do so because I do not know how to answer it. In the later writings of Aldous Huxley, in the latest poetry of T. S. Eliot you will find clues which may suggest an answer to the question. But whether an answer taken from the Catholic mysteries or an answer taken from the sacred books of the East satisfies you more will be purely a question of temperamental endowment.

I am fully aware that I have grazed a number of subjects and a number of philosophic systems without going very deeply into any of them. I will excuse myself by saying that my main concern has been to track down significant relations between one type of thinking and another, and to show how they cross-connect. If I have shown you that language has undergone a change in order to keep in line with cosmological inquiry (of which it forms a part) I shall feel more than satisfied.

At any rate I hope I have said enough to indicate the far-reaching changes in man's ideas about the outer universe. I want to turn now from outer to inner universe—to the domain of the psyche—for here also new ideas and discoveries can tell us something about Gerontion that perhaps he himself does not know.

## CHAPTER 3

## THE WORLD WITHIN

You mustn't look in my novel for the old stable ego of the character. There is another ego, according to whose action the individual is unrecognizable, which needs a deeper sense than any we've been used to exercise.

D. H. LAWRENCE

Do you know, I feel as though I were split in two? . . . It's just as though one's second self were standing beside one; one is sensible and rational oneself; but the other self is impelled to do something perfectly senseless.

DOSTOIEVSKI
*Notes from Underground*

WE have cleared some sort of space around the new ideas of time in order to examine their possible reaction upon the use of language. *Gerontion*, you remember, exhibits in its structure something like the pattern-behaviour of quanta. It does not progress along a line or a series of points, but in a new, a paradoxical way: it progresses by standing still. You leave Gerontion where you found him. *Ulysses* is, on the other hand, marked out like a race-course. The poem starts by giving you the idea, the characters, the location, the problem; then it proceeds to move forward towards a definite conclusion. The contrast in forms is an interesting one. *Ulysses* has a beginning, middle and end. *Gerontion* is simply there in a state of pure manifestation, so to speak.

To return to the historical method: while the outside view of things was changing under the impact of new ideas and discoveries in physics, the ego was also being explored, and it is in this context that we come upon the name of

Freud. The same forces which were inquiring into the structure of the universe were also busy extending the domains of our understanding within the boundaries of the self. Here, once more, we come upon discoveries and ideas which shaped and altered the use and application of language—and here again we shall examine only what is relevant to our subject—literature.

What sort of thing did people think the ego was before Freud came upon the scene? If the world was to consist of matter and mind, the self could only consist of mind and body. What was the mind?

Edgar Allen Poe, once writing to a friend about his æsthetic beliefs, gave the following picture of the ego:

> Dividing the world of mind into its three most imme-
> diately obvious distinctions, we have Pure Intellect, Taste
> and Moral Sense. . . . Just as the Intellect concerns itself with
> Truth, so Taste informs us of the Beautiful, while the Moral
> Sense is regardful of Duty.

These distinctions would not hold today, as you probably know. A little earlier Coleridge had made one of his oracular marginal notes in a book:

> Let a young man (he wrote) separate I from Me as far
> as he possibly can, and remove Me until it is almost lost in
> the remote distance. 'I am me' is as bad a fault in intellec-
> tuals and morals as it is in grammar, whilst none but one—
> God—can say 'I am I' or 'That I am'.

You will see from this that our thoughts about the self, the ego, had not advanced very far.

In the 1890's a couple of doctors called Freud and Breuer were studying hysteria and wondering how it was that under hypnosis a patient could recover painful experiences from his memory—experiences which in his waking state he did not remember. These experiences seemed to be stuck like thorns in some hidden part of the mind. That they caused the hysteria was becoming obvious, because their release under hypnosis seemed to have a healing effect on the hysteria. Was there, then, a part of the mind not accessible to conscious thought, where these unpleasant experiences lodged themselves? Was there an unconscious as well as a conscious part of the mind? That is how the idea of splitting the psyche first started. The Unconscious was born. They found that by hypnotizing the patient and making him discharge these festering secrets of his inner life they were performing a kind of catharsis for him. The secrets lost their sting, and his hysteria showed signs of improvement. They were making the contents of the hypothetical unconscious conscious: that was the way the two doctors began to formulate the idea.

Now Freud stumbled upon another curious fact. The so-called forgotten experiences were not really forgotten. This was proved on several occasions when he succeeded in getting the patient to remember them without hypnosis. It seemed as if the experiences in question had been, so to speak, bricked up in a corner of his mind. Some force inside himself had pressed them down and put them out of sight—because they were painful. Here there sprang to mind another idea. These thoughts were repressed—and so the conception of repression was born. Freud was using a new method of healing. He was releasing repressed thoughts which, when they came up to the surface and were accepted by the conscious mind, appeared to lose all their poisonous sting.

Pretty soon he found that another idea was emerging from his experiments—that of resistance. Naturally the patients' psyche was not willing to part with these painful experiences without a struggle. How, then, could one get round the brick wall of resistance which the psyche erected around these painful secrets? Freud was already dissatisfied with hypnosis and was anxious to discard it. Was there

any other way of digging into the secrets of the unconscious?

We do not know how the momentous idea first entered
his mind. His book *The Interpretation of Dreams* was published in 1900, and has been ever since the cornerstone of
the science known as psycho-analysis. In it he advanced a
theory which was entirely new to science, as well as to the
history of ideas. Dreams, he asserted, were a kind of language in which, under various poetical disguises, the
secrets of the unconscious could be discovered at work.
They were not just collections of nonsensical images, but
might be regarded as a kind of language.

The idea was that during sleep the unpleasant secrets
which were all bricked up in the unconscious managed to
sneak out and come to the surface. In order for them to
pass the censorship, so to speak, which the patient's self-
criticism and his moral attitude kept always on guard—in
order to slip past the guard they were got up in poetical
fancy-dress, they were disguised. If, added Freud, we
managed to discover the key to the dream language of the
individual we would be able to interpret his secret preoccupations. How successful the idea has been we all know.
Fifty years of psycho-analytical enquiry lie between the
publication date of that book and this lecture.

If Freud today is not as widely accepted as he should be
it is because of the moral tabu upon his concept of the
libido—and his belief that the nuclear structure of all
anxiety can be traced back to the sexual preoccupations of
childhood. So far his contention remains undisproved,
though the bias against it on the part of the ordinary man
(a product of his conditioning) shows little signs of yield-
ing.

Now as more and more dreams were collected and
analysed, and the preoccupations of more and more
patients classified, a new idea—a new series of ideas—
began to take shape in Freud's mind. He was trying, you

see, to bring to light the patient's secret preoccupations, but he was also most anxious to use this new method of study to discover, if possible, the structure of the psyche. What was a psyche? How did it grow? Was there something common to all psyches—or were they all hopelessly different?

As the enquiry progressed, despite the diversity and the complexity of the patient's preoccupations, he began to trace a kind of similar structure at the base of each and every one. In the first place the answers always led in the direction of early sexual experiences or sexual preoccupations, and in the second they always seemed to centre about the family relationship. Freud finally evolved a very poetical idea about the nuclear complex, as he calls it; the mother, father, child relationship was the key to it. This he called the Oedipus Complex from the myth of King Oedipus, who killed his father and won his mother as a wife. This story, he says, 'is only a slightly altered presentation of the infantile wish'. This complex, then, was the first great whirlpool which the infant psyche encountered and which it had to cross in order to reach adult life. Often the key to a successful adjustment in life could be traced back to preoccupations centring round this first crisis in the child's life.

We are only concerned with the by-products of psychoanalysis, in its effect on language and symbolism, so that it would not suit our purposes to study the theory in greater detail, or to go into the long battle between the different schools, which grew up around these discoveries. Certain aspects only are of interest to us.

While Freud had been finding a method of disentangling dreams and interpreting them another astonishing discovery came to light. The fantasies of his individual patients were often direct copies of race-myths and folk-tales of savage peoples. Psycho-analysis and anthropology joined hands at this point.

How was it that a twentieth century man, living in a modern city, was often found to be dreaming things which were being recorded as the myths or religious beliefs of some savage tribe in Africa? Was the myth, then, a kind of fantasy-product which enabled man to satisfy his desires, so to speak, in his imagination? If primitive myth was based on this idea, what about modern myth—what about modern art and religion? The analyst plunged into a study of these various subjects, using his knowledge of individual psychology to help him, and began to try and sketch in the general structure of man's history according to the terms of the new idea.

This department of psycho-analysis has provided us with some of the richest and most poetical thinking of the twentieth century, and it is a thousand pities that these books are all dressed up in a heavy clinical terminology because the ideas in them are of relevance and interest to all of us. Nobody who has a child today, for example, can properly enjoy and understand the experience unless he knows something of the unconscious mechanisms behind the ideas of play, of guilt, of love—subjects which have been illuminated by this great new science. Similarly nobody who reads Freud carefully and honestly, referring the main ideas of this great thinker back to his own life, his own fears and preoccupations, will find anything but strength and relief from them. The name Freud means 'Joy', and in time he will be recognized in the world as a real joy-bringer. His ideas have allowed us access to a new territory inside ourselves in which each one of us who is seeking to grow, to identify himself more fully with life, will feel like Columbus discovering America. But to appreciate him fully two things are necessary: freedom from prejudice, and a desire to face the truth.

The connection, then, between racial myths and individual dreams—a connection still being explored—yielded a vast new tract of knowledge. But meanwhile investigations into the structure of the dream were continuing. Among other relations we might mention the space and time aspect of dreams:

> The dream always turns temporal relations into spatial ones whenever it has to deal with them. Thus, one may see in a dream a scene between people who look very small and far away, as if one were looking at them through the wrong end of a pair of opera glasses. The smallness and the spatial remoteness here mean the same; it is remoteness in time that is meant, the interpretation being that it is a scene from the far distant past.

So the dream has its own attitude to space and time! And herein lies a mystery which as yet has not been cleared up. I would like to give it to you in Freud's own words:*

> The laws of logic—above all, the law of contradiction—do not hold for processes in the Id. Contradictory impulses exist side by side without neutralizing each other or drawing apart; at most they combine in compromise-formations under the overpowering economic pressure towards discharging their energy. There is nothing in the Id which can be compared to negation, and we are astonished to find in it an exception to the philosopher's assertion that space and time are necessary forms of our mental acts. In the Id there is nothing corresponding to the idea of time, no recognition of the passage of time, and (a thing which is very remarkable and awaits adequate attention in philosophic thought) no alteration of mental processes by the passage of time. Conative impulses which have never got beyond the Id, and even impressions which have been pushed down into the Id by repression, are virtually immortal and are preserved for whole decades as though they had only recently occurred. . . . It is constantly being borne in upon me that we have made far too little use of our theory of the indubitable fact that the repressed remains unaltered by the passage of time. This seems to offer us the possibility of an approach to some really profound truths. But I myself have made no further progress here.

55

Beyond pointing out the passage dealing with contradictory processes co-existing, and also the fact that Freud uses the phrase 'discharge of energy' which he has borrowed from electricity, I would prefer to leave the quotation without comment. It deserves the most serious consideration, however, from all of us, for it gives one another aspect of the time-problem.

But what of the interpretation of dreams? For Freud the dream 'is a pathological product, the first member of the series which includes the hysterical symptom, the obsession and the delusion among its members. . . .' You will see from this that Freud's system is based very firmly upon the idea of causation. The repressed impulse, looking for an escape hatch, chooses the poetical mechanism in order to escape. But the linguistic expression of the dream is peculiar to itself. Let me once again give you Freud's words rather than my own:

All the verbal apparatus by means of which the more subtle thought-relations are expressed, the conjunctions and prepositions, the variations of declension and conjugation, are lacking, because the means of portraying them are absent: just as in primitive grammarless speech only the raw material of thought can be expressed, and the abstract is merged again in the concrete from which it sprang. What is left over may very well seem to lack coherence. It is as much the result of the archaic regression in the mental apparatus as of the demands of the censorship that so much use is made of the representation of certain objects and processes by means of symbols which have become strange to conscious thought.

But of more far-reaching import are the other alterations to which the elements comprising the dream-thoughts are subjected. Such of them as have any point of contact are *condensed* into new unities. . . . It is as if a force were at work which subjected the material to a process of pressure or squeezing together. As a result of condensation one element in a manifest dream may correspond to a number of elements of the dream-thoughts; but conversely one of the elements from among the dream-thoughts may be represented by a number of pictures in the dream.

Even more remarkable is the other process of *displacement* or transference of accent which in conscious thinking figures only as an error in thought or as a method employed in jokes.

I must apologize for so long a quotation. But if one reads it over carefully one gets, I think, a very clear picture of how the dream works. It is like ordinary language transposed into a new key, unfamiliar at first, but with practice not so difficult to read. Recently in a novel I came across an excellent example to illustrate the manner in which the dream symbolizes things. There was a man depicted as getting into bed after a heavy day's work. His conscience was bothering him because he had had a quarrel with a friend. Someone had said: 'Why don't you telephone him this evening when you get back from work and smooth the whole thing out?' The idea had remained in his mind—he intended to smooth the quarrel out—but after dinner he felt so tired that he went straight to bed. As he was falling off to sleep he had a half-waking dream in which he saw himself, with a plane in his hand, planing a piece of wood smooth—in other words, of course, 'smoothing out' the misunderstanding symbolically.

But dreams are not all as easy as this one to interpret. Sometimes they are projected in a manner so inextricably confused that they remind us of those thousand fragments of a Greek vase which the archæologist's patience assembles into a single and beautiful whole. The dream takes the short cut across the accepted linguistic relations —just as *Gerontion* does. Our test of the dream, as of the modern poem, is the law of association. But before we speak of this let us illustrate the idea by making up a simple dream and breaking it down again, in order to examine the relationship of the various parts to the whole. This might give us some sort of clue to the way a modern poem is written.

Let us suppose that a man goes to bed with several different problems on his mind. Let us make a list of the problems and construct the dream around them. Say:

(a) That he has had a quarrel with a business partner and in the course of it he was told he was a 'Judas' who was betraying his partner's trust. This was today.

(b) That he is feeling guilty because he has been unfaithful to his wife. It is the third time he has done this. It happened last week.

(c) He promised to assist a friend of his, Peter Cook, over a difficult financial period, but has not bothered to do so. He has been expecting a message from Cook for the last three weeks.

Let us imagine that these three preoccupations, all having taken place at different times, choose to get jumbled into a dream. They might emerge like this:

### THE DREAM

He was standing in the lobby of a large hotel, which he recognized as the Grand Hotel, London. A man in a page's uniform came out of the lift and walked towards him as if to deliver a message. When he got close he saw that he was not a page at all. It was a large bird, a cock, dressed in the page's uniform, which clapped its wings three times and crowed. The bird was wearing a chef's hat. He woke up.

At first glance this looks a fantastic and inextricable collection of rubbish, impossible to sort or rearrange into a coherent message. Yet strangely enough the symbols, taken one by one, can be made to fit into a general pattern. By asking our patient what each symbol reminds him of, and collecting his associations, we might get something like the following message from the dream:

(a) The Hotel reminds him of a hotel where he met a woman by arrangement, and where his third infidelity was committed. In the dream it was called The Grand Hotel, but in reality its name was The Little Spa Hotel. The dream often substitutes the opposite of what it wants to say as a disguise.

(b) The cock crowed thrice: that reminds him of Peter who denied Christ three times. It also reminds him that he was called 'Judas' this morning by his business partner. He has introduced Peter because of 'thrice'—the number of times he has betrayed his wife.

(c) Why should it be a cock—and moreover a cock with a chef's hat on its head? The association 'chef' leads him to Cook, the name of the man from whom he has been expecting a message. The dream often makes puns on words like this. So that the idea of betraying Cook has also got mixed up with the two other betrayals—that of his business partner and his wife.

Thus the three distinct lines of thought have been compressed into a single brief picture flashed upon the screen of his dream-life; the three different betrayals, all distinct, are present but in a squeezed-up form. We have only scratched the surface of the dream, of course, with this rough and ready explanation. The more you examine it, and the more you learn of the associations which surround each symbol, the richer and more varied the content becomes. We have not yet 'analysed' the page. We have not yet noticed that the intrusion of Peter into the scheme is also an echo of the name of the man from whom he expected the message—Peter Cook—as well as the man who betrayed Christ. The dream, then, operates upon a series of different levels, and if we once dispose of the top layer of associations we find another layer and another underneath, packed like chocolates.

The first 'hotel' association may be connected with this infidelity that is worrying him, but if he goes on thinking about it a hundred and one other memories will come to mind, and before he knows where he is, he will be back in his childhood. Over our early childhood, says Freud, lies a veil. He adds:

> You know it is one of the tasks of analysis to lift the veil of amnesia which shrouds the earliest years of childhood and to bring the expression of infantile sexuality hidden behind it into the conscious mind. . . . Now these first sexual experiences of the child are bound up with painful impressions of anxiety, prohibition, disappointment and punishment. One can understand why they have been repressed; but, if so, it is difficult to see why they should have such easy access to the dream-life, why they should provide the pattern for so many dream-fantasies . . .

Our dream, then, of which we have only examined the surface, contains depths. Who knows where the chef's hat or the name Peter Cook may lead us if we follow it down the long winding corridors of association? We must be content to examine it in terms of communication, and ask ourselves whether in a modern poem something like the same dislocation of syntax and continuity is not effected. Let us take a line from the poet W. H. Auden:

O love, the interest itself in thoughtless Heaven.

Can we apply something like the same associative criteria to it as we have applied to the dream we have just analysed? It is worth trying. Let us then ask ourselves what it means despite its oracular appearance. I assume that a number of similar ideas from different contexts (like the

different times but the same idea of betrayal in the dream)
are compressed together in one phrase. If we take the
word 'interest' for example, it at once branches off into
various meanings:

*Interest*

| Interest | self-interest | interest on capital |
| curiosity | self-love | compound interest |
| | selfishness | |

If we take the primary meaning of the phrase and paraphrase it we might reach something like this: 'O love, there
is no reward for you in Heaven, as we were once told.
Heaven is not thinking about us. Love is its own reward.'
This would give us the meaning of the phrase 'the interest
itself'. In other words 'its own reward'. And 'thoughtless
Heaven' would be the heaven which does not reckon up
our acts, and find out how many were good, how many
were bad. Heaven is beyond the moral judgment. On the
other hand, there are associations flowing the other way—
stock-exchange associations, so to speak. They come from
the word interest. 'Doing good is not a question of banking
in order to draw a dividend on Heaven later on. You are
not investing money in a bank. If you act with love, and
without thought of the reward, you will find that love is its
own repayment.'

I have said enough, I hope, to indicate what a formidable piece of compression lies behind a simple statement
today in poetry. If the tasks of appreciation have increased,
however, so has our knowledge of the structure and application of language to ideas. More than this, the values of
the individual word have more than doubled their significance, a fact which is entirely due to the researches of
psycho-analysts among the data of anthropology. Let
me give you an example of how this kind of research has
gone behind the dictionary meaning of words and touches

the symbolic sources from which the word springs. I quote
from Dr. Groddeck's *The World of Man*:

The very word sex suggests the violent splitting asunder
of humanity into male and female. Sexus is derived from
secare, to cut, from which we also get segmentum, a part cut
from a circle. It conveys the idea that man and woman once
formed a unity, that together they make a complete whole,
the perfect circle of the individuum, and that both sections
share the properties of this individuum. These suggestions
are, of course, in harmony with the ancient Hebrew legend;
which told how God first created a human being who was
both male and female, Adam-Lilith, and later sawed it
asunder. We find a similar idea in the writings of Plato. The
verb secare, to cut, is related to hosts of others through which
it is not easy to clear a path. To take a few at random—both
sickle and scythe are cognate with secare. Both are tradi-
tionally associated with the image of death. Probably the
sickle is the more primitive of the two; in any case it is richer
in symbolic associations. The sickle-moon is so called because of its shape, and since the term is used only of the
moon when it is waxing it gives to Death the suggestion not
of annihilation but of a new birth.

This should show you that by the time we reach the
tribal associations of a word we are in the midst of a jungle
of symbols. Neither anthropology nor psychology is quite
clear of it as yet—but in this context I should speak of Dr.
Jung and his modifications of Freudian theory; for it is he
who developed a new attitude to psycho-analysis: Jung is
the Plato of psycho-analysis. Freud's discoveries face forwards into the twentieth century, but his working-methods
and his intellectual predispositions faced backwards towards Darwin. The psyche became a sort of impulse-and-
inhibition machine—for Freud was a mechanist at heart—
and as psycho-analysis proceeded to branch out, and over-
flow into various other departments of speculation like
anthropology, æsthetics, religion, some of the younger men
began to become uneasy about it. Freud, you see, could

not for a moment drop his strict inherence to causation. He was looking for primary causes. It was Jung, one of his pupils, who developed a new attitude to the science, which we might describe as vitalist in outlook. Jung substituted the idea of creative balance for the idea of first cause. While he still used Freud's methods, he redefined many of his terms, among them the 'libido' idea—which for Freud meant a totality of sexual desire. He developed his own terms of reference, and redefined his objectives. For him treatment became, not a pure cause and effect operation, but a spiritual reintegration. In the course of this readjustment he went very deeply into the question of fantasy and myth, and instead of simply explaining them in terms of one or other of the Freudian beliefs, he tried to give them relevance and meaning for the patient's psyche. Francis J. Mott has carried many of these ideas forward towards a new system of knowledge.

We have not time to go into Jung's wonderful revaluation of the Freudian apparatus, nor to study the contributions made by Dr. Adler, another great analyst, as well as a host of others. The point I want to make is that the symbolic apparatus of the artist received a new charge, a new accretion of power from all this knowledge. He became aware that the symbols he was using were far richer than he had known. In fact they were so rich that he found himself in difficulties with them. Out of these Freudian findings, too, another thing was becoming clear—that words in the unconscious were double in meaning, just as so many of the impulses were double. How could you use, for example, the word 'sex' to mean 'uniting, joining' when you were reminded that it was derived from the idea of cutting asunder, of separating? To this we must attribute a certain amount of the artist's apparent ambiguity. His symbols were developing a multiple impact. Up to now they had been more or less fixed within the limits of their dictionary meaning. Therefore the whole structure of his

language began to change under him—and today the
character of art suggests that the artist has replaced the
idea of causation with an idea of balance, of fulcrum. If, as
investigation suggested, the psyche was really a bisexual
thing, if moreover qualities often indicated their opposite
in the unconscious—'fear always conceals a wish', 'sentimentality is suppressed brutality'—what was to happen to
the clear outlines of formal statement?

Herein I believe lies the key to the new influences creep-
ing into art—influences which may be recognized in the
Eastern philosophies which are being studied by writers as
diverse as Huxley, Heard, Isherwood, Maugham. For
does not the Bhagvad-Gita and the Book of the Simple
Way enjoin the reader to 'free himself of the opposites'?
Each of us however will have to follow up this aspect of
things for himself.

Analysis, as you see, had done all that had been expected of it. But to analyse is to delimit. If you pick a hole
in a woollen sweater you can go on unwinding the wool
until—you have no longer a sweater in your hands but a
ball of wool. The orthodoxy of the Freudian practitioner
centred about the causation-idea. It led to a rigidity of
outlook which one finds much modified by Jung, Adler
and Rank. The original attitude to the psyche has been
undergoing a further change. It is not a mechanism any
longer but an organism.

One dares not assert that poets and writers were consciously aware of this gradual trend in ideas and of the
gradual modifications of our thoughts about the universe
or ourselves. Poetry is the raw material of sensibility, and
the poet's job is to go on making poetry, not to think too
much about why or wherefore. But poets belong to an
age. They have ancestors and pedigrees like their poems.
And they register the general drift of things by their
work.

I am suggesting that the literature of our age is distinguished by two sorts of compression which reflect both the changes in the idea of time—which make poets present their material not as argument but as direct and instantaneous statement, impressionistically—and also the change in our attitude to the psyche. Thus you find not only the ideas of a poem compressed but the sound-values as well, with the rhyme often coming in the middle of the line instead of being set like a milestone at the end of every five stresses. Further compression still (as in James Joyce's last work) leads to the pun—the word with more than one meaning, like 'funferal' which is his way of transposing the word 'funeral'. In fact the type of language which Joyce chose to express himself in when he wrote *Finnegan's Wake* is a kind of *reductio ad absurdum* of the new influences. Compression, like analysis, can only go so far. The pendulum is already swinging back in the direction of simpler statement and purer sound. But it can only do so when all these ideas have been thoroughly assimilated and digested.

I have described these ideas at some length because I believe them to be a key to our way of looking at things, and a help in discussing modern works like *Ulysses* or *Sons and Lovers*. Do not imagine, however, that the final meaning of a work of art lies in any explanation of it. Yet sometimes a poetical explanation can illuminate something for us—but it is always something in us, and not in the work we seek to understand. Thus though the theory of the Oedipus Complex is a beautiful one and fits many of the facts of the case we must not imagine that it disposes either of art or the artist. Freud himself, in his essay on Dostoievski, says: 'Before the problem of the creative artist analysis must lay down its arms'. Freud was too great and too honest a thinker not to recognize the limitations of analytical thought itself.

Before we leave the subject it is necessary to examine the terms of reference of the Oedipus Complex briefly. We have seen how for Freud this is the 'nuclear complex' of our lives. It is also, he claims, the subject matter of much of the greatest art; he writes:

> It can scarcely be mere coincidence that three of the masterpieces of the literature of all time, the *Oedipus Rex* of Sophocles, Shakespeare's *Hamlet* and Dostoievski's *The Brothers Karamazov*, should all deal with the same subject, a father's murder. In all three the motive for the deed, sexual rivalry for the woman, is laid bare. The most straightforward is certainly the representation in the drama built upon the Greek legend. In it the hero himself commits the crime . . . etc.

Art criticism, in terms of the Oedipus Complex, has produced some extremely valuable and intelligent literature. Freud himself has done a masterly study of Leonardo da Vinci and Dostoievski, while Ernest Jones has made an exhaustive study of Hamlet's inhibitions in the light of his mother-father relationship. If indeed this nuclear complex is the basis upon which our profoundest art-works are built what is to be the subject-matter of the future? Presumably by making the mechanism of this complex conscious Freud has deprived the artist of his greatest subject-matter, deprived him of a source-book of suffering upon which to draw for emotional material? Can a public which has been instructed into the meaning of this basic pattern, this source of early suffering, ever enjoy its Hamlets any more? It is a question I leave to critics bolder than myself.

Here again I suggest we see that the contemporary artist, having reached the end of a subjective cycle in Lawrence, Joyce, (though we might carry the story as far forward as Henry Miller) is turning his face away from autobiographical form. We might even say that a new note of transcendental moralism has begun to creep into his work. Whether his belief is orthodox or not, there is a distinct emergence of moral preoccupation in the new poetry of Eliot and Auden, while Huxley has so far become a propagandist for the Perennial Philosophy that it has completely paralysed him as an artist. Just as the analyst has replaced the idea of cause and effect (as an end in itself) with the idea of creative balance, so the modern artist is shouldering his responsibility as a creature entangled in opposites which it is his business to resolve in the interests of the general pattern.

We have traced, in very sketchy fashion, to be sure, the curve between the objectivity of Tennyson's *Ulysses* and the exhausted subjectivity of Eliot's *Gerontion*, and found, I hope, a few reasons for their differing attitude, outlook and manners. Between *Gerontion* and the *Four Quartets* stretches another great curve of sensibility with different characteristics. When you come to the verse-plays of Eliot, and begin to study one called *The Family Reunion*, my question about the effect of the Oedipus Complex as a fund of emotional material should arise in your mind once more—for Eliot has attempted to rewrite Hamlet: an attempt, in my humble opinion, which has not completely come off. Is it because the artist could not compass his theme—or is the theme no longer of sufficient value to the artist? Each will have to decide this question for himself.

If we are to consider modern literature, however, as if the term meant something, we should offer a line of demarcation after which the full impact of these ideas began to be felt. Where would it fall? I would suggest that the accent might be placed somewhere between 1918—the end of the Great War—and 1925. But the briefest chronological survey would show just how tangled the web is, and how the various strands of influence and development are woven together. In the year 1919 for example we have Masefield's *Reynard the Fox*—a triumph of the naturalistic method, to place beside H. G. Wells' *Outline*

*of History*. In 1920 *In Chancery* by Galsworthy appeared
and was backed by D. H. Lawrence's *Women in Love*,
Conrad's *The Rescue*, George Moore's *Héloïse and Abélard*
and Katherine Mansfield's *Bliss*. In this year also the
poets were to be found studying the first Hopkins collection, the first collected poems of de La Mare and the tense
beautifully controlled war-poems of Wilfred Owen. In
1921 come Aldous Huxley's *Crome Yellow* and de La
Mare's *Memoirs of a Midget*.

In all this diversity of purpose and expression dare we
seek for a unifying cause among the ideas which we have
so far touched upon? Not until 1922, I think, though the
ferment must have been going on below the surface. But
in 1922 we stumble upon *The Waste Land* of T. S. Eliot,
which altered the whole face of poetry, and *Ulysses* by
James Joyce, whose technical innovations were to alter
the face of prose—in neither case, however, for the
better.

The war between experiment and tradition which had
been smouldering since before the war, crystallized somewhere here and took shape from the attitudes and anxieties
of the post-war world. And yet, in order to indicate how
faulty the historical attitude is we should not forget that in
this year, too, *Hassan* by James Elroy Flecker was
launched, though six years after its author's death. But
we may immediately reassure ourselves by recalling the
publication of Virginia Woolf's *Jacob's Room* in the same
year. Most of the new findings of our age can be seen
reflected in these experimentalists. Poetry and prose alike
began to borrow the colours of the dream, and the new
ideas of time can be seen in the loosening causal connec-
tions of the action. Even in D. H. Lawrence, the surface
of whose prose still reflected the order of traditional
methods, we can see an attempt to grasp a new attitude to
the ego. 'You mustn't look in my novel for the old stable
ego,' he writes, and adds that he is following his characters

through 'allotropic states' to establish not how they act but what they are, essentially.

The decades of the present century (sums up the Cambridge English Literature) have been chiefly remarkable for the breaches made in the usually accepted frontiers between the physical and metaphysical realms. Philosophers now explain psychological phenomena in physical terms; physicists give metaphysical interpretations of natural phenomena. The future historian of modern literature will find it difficult to separate science and philosophy into distinct chapters. The century began with Planck's 'quantum theory' . . . the first promulgation of Einstein's theory of relativity followed; and the physical concepts that had seemed as firm as the earth itself began to grow unsubstantial. . . . No more could we think of 'space' and 'time' as separate entities: we were compelled to think in terms of a space-time continuum. The idea was not entirely new. . . . Alice, in continual perplexity about her varied extensions in space, i.e. about her changing universe, and the Mad Hatter, convinced that 'time' was not 'it' but 'him' (and therefore dimensional), may be taken as parables of anticipation.

The conditions of history as we see it, from our position in time, appear to illustrate two sorts of principles working in opposition. The vitalist and the mechanist attitudes to the world: and attitudes well enough illustrated in the kind of opposing temperaments which, since the beginning of history, have imposed their ideas upon it. The gap between Plato and Aristotle as temperaments gives a good example, from the highest realm, of this division. It is a division which repeats itself through history in all the sciences, in art and in literature, and which has for generations bogged the critic down among such opposing terms as 'Classic and Romantic' or 'Reason and Mysticism'. It is unlikely that the war between the two will ever be resolved unless applied biology succeeds in conditioning both critics and the public into uniformity!

To us, living in the fifties, it seems that the pendulum has swung out very far in the direction of the 'romantic' or the 'mystical'. We are probably in the midst of reaction still, yet it seems clear that the respect for the Noumenal world as against the Phenomenal is receiving every day a fresh impetus. Cosmology, in an attempt to remain inclusive of the so-called 'known facts of science', finds itself all but joining hands with those who favour a deeply mystical view of the world. And it is poetic justice indeed that science itself is responsible for so many ideas that sound fantastic to us—and would have sounded completely incomprehensible to our grandfathers. Nevertheless their foundation, when all is said and done, is observable fact.

Meanwhile the study of the occult sciences which began in the 1870's and which seemed to run for a while underground, like a river, has surfaced again and brought a renewed interest in the wisdom of Eastern religions and Eastern attitudes to thought and belief. It is as if the arts and sciences were converging steadily upon a new attitude to life—as yet out of sight—but an attitude which might have the sanction of the realistic physicist no less than the mystic, and the religious conformist who claims that the Christian attitude has its place also as an impetus towards the Perennial Philosophy. One such philosophy I have already mentioned. In the works of Francis J. Mott a new sort of synthesis is sketched which offers hope for a future in which man can acccommodate these different faculties into a new type of thinking—a sort of religious materialism.

We cannot hope to follow all the roads within the small scope of these lectures. But we can perhaps look at one example of the great change towards vitalism in the attitude of psychology. I will not choose Jung who, since the death of Freud, must be regarded as the greatest living psychologist, for the complexity and beauty of his system would need more time, space and paper than we have at our disposal.

I would prefer to choose a psychologist who, though he is not well known, illustrates in his life and thought the new vitalist attitude to the ego and its problems. You will see from his system how far we have travelled from the mechanistic attitude of Freud.

## CHAPTER 4

# BEYOND THE EGO?

There is however one question which touches our subject, and which only a psychologist could answer. But let us ask it. Will the creative process alter? Will the mirror get a new coat of quicksilver? In other words can human nature change? . . . All I will do is to state a possibility. If human nature does alter it will be because individuals manage to look at themselves in a new way. Here and there people—a very few people, but a few novelists are among them—are trying to do this. Every institution and vested interest is against such a search: organized religion, the State, the family in its economic aspect, have nothing to gain. . . .

E. M. FORSTER: *Aspects of the Novel*

The neurotic is himself a symptom of the modern conflict between the individual and society, a conflict which might in other ages have been productively surmounted in artistic creation. Nowadays the old art-ideology is no longer, and the new personality-idea not yet, strong enough to admit either solution for the individual impulse to create. Everyone suffers—individual, community, and, not least, art as an ideological expression of their interrelation.

OTTO RANK: *Art and Artist*

The creative men of our time are not capable of going the whole way and accepting the development of their personality as the truly creative problem. What hinders them is the same individual feeling of guilt which in earlier times was able, owing to the counter-force of religious submissiveness, to work itself out creatively, but nowadays limits both complete artistic creation and complete personality-development. For artistic creation has, in the course of its development, changed from a means for the furtherance of the culture of the community into a means for the construction of personality.

OTTO RANK: *Art and Artist*

THE work of Georg Walther Groddeck* (1866-1934) is hardly known at all outside the professional circles in which he spent his whole working life as a doctor. Yet he was held in great esteem by his fellow psycho-analysts and his patients, while his various books have been translated into English and have won for him a small following in medical circles as well as among ordinary readers who are interested in out-of-the-way literature. He is, I think, a suitable subject of study for us, first because his system (if we can call it that) is simple, and lends itself to an easy summary (whereas that of Jung or Adler would need hours and pages of exposition): secondly because he is the first analyst to try to go beyond the ego in his conception of human personality. When we come to study the later poetry of Eliot and Auden we will find this attitude useful in helping us to form some sort of picture of the reality which they are trying to describe. In Groddeck we reach the boundaries of the ego and are allowed to peer into the mystical regions which lie beyond, while his work illustrates just how far the pendulum has swung from the mechanist view to the vitalist. We might describe him as the complete vitalist.

Freud saw the psyche as an intricate two-piece mechanism, consisting of conscious and unconscious. To Groddeck the ego and its works were functions of something else. In his work he applied analysis, for the most part, to organic disease, and his claims deserve attention. Though his apparatus is Freudian, and though he never ceases to acclaim Freud publicly for what he was—a genius—yet his conception of the psyche is a totally different one. Where Freud spoke of analysis in regard to the psyche the early vitalists like Jung preferred to think in terms of creative synthesis. Groddeck went a step further than this. His concept of disease is metaphysical. He thinks in terms of liberation—to use a word inherited from the mystic schools. His books form a convenient intersecting point between religion, art and science: and his philosophy is a simple if radical one. Groddeck believes in what he calls 'The It'. . . .

The sum total of an individual human being, physical, mental and spiritual, the organism with all its forces, the microcosmos, the universe which is a man, I conceive of as self unknown and forever unknowable, and I call this 'The It', as the most indefinite term available without either emotional or intellectual associations. The It-hypothesis I regard, not as a truth,—for what do any of us know about absolute Truth?—but as a useful tool in work and life; it has stood the test of years of medical work and experiment and so far nothing has happened which would lead me to abandon it or even to modify it in any essential degree. I assume that man is animated by the It which directs what he does and what he goes through, and that the assertion 'I live' only expresses a small and superficial part of the total experience 'I am lived by the It' . . .

For Freud, as indeed for the civilization of which he was both representative and part, the ego is paramount. It was a box which Freud's ingenuity divided and subdivided into component parts as every new discovery came to light. Groddeck considered the ego a mere mask which deluded the human being into thinking that he was responsible for what he was.

When we occupy ourselves in any way either with ourselves or with our fellow-man, we think of the ego as the essential thing . . . We know, for instance, that no man's ego has had anything to do with the fact that he possesses a human form, that he is a human being. Yet as soon as we perceive in the distance a being who is walking on two legs we immediately assume that this being is an ego, that he can be made responsible for what he is and what he does, and indeed if we did not do this everything that is human would disappear from the world. Still we know quite certainly that the humanity of this being was never willed by his ego. . . . What has breathing to do with the will? We have to begin

as soon as we leave the womb, we cannot choose but breathe
. . . No one has command over the power to sleep. It will
come or it will not. No one can regulate the beating of his
heart. . . .

Man, then, is a function of this mysterious force which
expresses itself through him, through his illness no less than
his health. For Groddeck the psycho-analytic equipment
is merely a lens which will help him see a little more deeply
into the motives behind illness. The causes of sickness or
health, he decided, were unknown. Disease appeared to
be one of the psyche's ways of expressing itself, that was all.
In all the marvellous pages of Freud we see the analytical
intellect pursuing its chain of cause-and-effect; if only the
last link can be reached, if only the first cause can be
established, the whole pattern will become clear. Freud
believed that science could reach that cause by thought
and experiment. To Groddeck such a proposition was
false. The Whole was an unknown, a forever unknowable
entity whose shadows and functions we are. Only a small
corner of this territory was free to be explored by the
watchful, only the fringes of this universe could fall within
the finite comprehension of the human mind. Analysis for
him was not a hunt for causes pure and simple. He used it
as a sort of mental windscreen-wiper, which cleared away
the delusions of the ego about its own constitution, and
enabled the psyche to get a glimpse at the mystery behind. In the domain of theory Groddeck was Freud's
admiring and deeply attentive pupil, but, as you can see,
he was using analysis for ends far greater than Freud
himself could perceive.

However unlikely it may seem it is nevertheless a fact that
any sort of treatment, scientific or old-wives' poultices, may
turn out to be right for the patient, since the outcome of
medical or other treatment is not determined by the means
prescribed but by what the patient's It likes to make of the —

prescription. If this were not the case then every broken limb which had been properly set and bandaged would be bound to heal, whereas every surgeon knows of obstinate cases which despite all care and attention defy his efforts and refuse to heal. It is my opinion . . . that a beneficent influence may be directed upon the injured parts . . . by psycho-analysing the general Unconscious: indeed I believe that every sickness of the organism, whether physical or mental, may be influenced by psycho-analysis . . . although of course a man with pneumonia must be put immediately to bed and kept warm, a gangrened limb must be amputated, a broken bone set and immobilized . . . a badly built house may have to be pulled down and reconstructed with all possible speed where no alternative accommodation is available, and the architect who built it so badly must be made to see his mistakes . . . and an It which has damaged its own work, lung or bone . . . must learn its lesson and avoid such mistakes in future.
. .

You will see from this passage to what a degree the old mind-and-body controversy of the Victorians has been undermined. This is largely due to Freud's discoveries about the effect of psychic troubles upon organic functions. But the whole weight of responsibility is thrown, not upon a hypothetical cause, an abstraction, but upon the patient's own unconscious. Groddeck goes on to discuss his diagnostic methods as follows:

Since everything has at least two sides, however, it can always be considered from two points of view, and so it is my custom to ask a patient who has slipped and broken his arm: '*What was your idea in breaking your arm?*' Whereas if anyone is reported to have had recourse to morphia to get sleep the night before, I ask him: '*How was it that the idea of morphine became so important yesterday that you made yourself sleepless in order to have an excuse for taking it?*' So far I have never failed to get a useful reply to such questions and there is nothing extraordinary about that, for if we take the trouble to search we can always find an inward and an outward cause for any event in life.

Groddeck practised medicine, then, according to a new idea of healing. The virtue of his methods for us lies in the literary charm and simplicity with which he has described them in his books. He steered clear of the dangers of too much terminology, too much intellectual supercargo, which still weighs down the armature of Jung's ideas, and makes him often difficult to read for any but the professional medical man. Groddeck's humour, self-deprecating irony and style commend him to the common reader straight away, and force one to wonder why he is not better known. It is true that he is unorthodox, that he renounces science as such. 'It is in vain,' says Freud somewhere, 'that Groddeck protests he has nothing to do with science'. In vain. For Groddeck influenced Freud, who paid him the compliment of borrowing his It-concept and hopelessly misinterpreting it. Freud did not see beyond the ego, and was consequently led to situate the It within the confines of the ego itself—as a sort of primitive subself below the surface of the higher nature of man. It is very unsatisfactory. But Groddeck loved Freud too well to protest at this.

Health and sickness are among the It's forms of expression always ready for use. Consideration of these two modes of expression reveals the remarkable fact that the It never uses either of them alone, but always both at once: that is to say no one is altogether ill, there is always some part which remains sound even in the worst illnesses: and no one is altogether well, there is always something wrong, even in the perfectly healthy. Perhaps the best comparison we could give would be a pair of scales. The It toys with the scales putting a weight now in the right pan, now in the left, but never leaving either pan empty; this game, which is often puzzling but always significant, never purposeless, is what we know as life. If once the It loses interest in the game it lets go of life and dies. Death is always voluntary; no one dies except he has desired death. . . . The It is ambivalent, making mysterious but deep-meaning play with will and counter-will . . . driving the sick man into a dual relation with his doctor so that he loves him as his best friend and helper, yet sees in him a menace to that artistic effort, his illness.

Illness, then, for Groddeck is something like bad meta-physics, and by uncovering the secrets of the It in psycho-analysis he alters, so to speak, the direction and purpose of its activity—he alters the whole fulcrum of the psyche. With Freud we penetrate more deeply into the cognative process. With Groddeck we learn the mystery of partici-pation with a world of which we are part and from which the pretensions of the ego have sought to amputate us. The difference is a radical one.

What then of health and disease? They have become purely relative expressions. Groddeck does not try to trace their sources. He suggests that the processes of the It can sometimes be influenced. But it is always the preten-sions of the ego which constitute the main target of the attack.

> I do maintain that man creates his own illnesses for a definite purpose, using the outer world merely as an instru-ment, finding there an inexhaustible supply of material which he can use for this purpose, to-day a piece of orange-peel, to-morrow the spirochete of syphilis, the day after a draught of cold air, or anything else that will help him to pile up his woes. And always to gain pleasure, no matter how unlikely that may seem, for every human being experiences something of pleasure in suffering; every human being has the feeling of guilt and tries to get rid of it by self-punish-ment.

You will see from the above quotation how deep a debt in method Groddeck owes to Freud—but you will also see his own particular orientation towards life and healing. And what of the It? Groddeck says there is no such thing. He is most careful to insist that the It is not a thing-in-itself, but merely a way of seeing, a convenient rule-of-thumb hypothesis for attacking the ego under its various disguises. In this his philosophy bears a close resemblance to the Chinese Tao-concept, which manifests itself in endless dualities. The It is a Way, not a Thing. Having persuaded you to accept this, Groddeck is prepared to try a half-length sketch of it.

Some moment of beginning must be supposed for this hypothetical It, and for my own purposes I quite arbitrarily suppose it to start with fertilization . . . and I assume that the It comes to an end with the death of the individual. . . . Now the hypothetical It-unit . . . contains within itself two It-units, a male and a female. . . . The two then divide again into four, into eight, into sixteen and so on, until there comes to be what we commonly designate a human being. . . . Now in the fertilized ovule, minute as it is, there must be something or other (the It, we have assumed?) which is able to take charge of this multitudinous dividing into cells, to give them all distinctive forms and functions, to induce them to group themselves as skin, bones, eyes, ears, brain. What becomes of the original It in the moment of division? It must obviously impart its powers to the cells into which it divides, since we know that each of them is able to exist and redivide independently of each other. . . . It must not be forgotten that the brain, and therefore the intellect, is itself created by the It. . . . Long before the brain comes into existence the It of man is already active and 'thinking' without the brain, since it must first construct the brain before it can use it to think with. This is a fundamental point and one that we are apt to ignore or forget. . . .

The It, then, antedates all our intellectual apparatus, our conceptual mechanism. It is later, with the growth of the ego, that we persuade ourselves that our reasoning powers belong to our personality as private property; meanwhile the ego-It relationship is a source of confusion.

Over and against the It stands the ego, the I, which I take to be merely the tool of the It, but which we are forced to regard as the It's master, for whatever we say in theory there remains always for us men the final verdict 'I am I' . . . We cannot get away from it, and even while I assert the proposition to be false I am obliged to act as if it were true. Yet I am by no means I, but only a continuously changing form in which my 'It' displays itself, and the 'I' feeling is just one of its many ways of deceiving the conscious mind and making it a pliant tool . . . I go so far as to believe that every single separate cell has this consciousnesss of individuality, every tissue, every organic system. In other words every It-unit can deceive itself, if it likes, into thinking of itself as an individuality, a person, an I. This is all very confusing, but there it is . . . I cannot prove this, of course, but as a doctor I believe it, for I have seen how the stomach can respond to certain amounts of nourishment, how it makes careful use of its secretions according to the nature and quantity of the material supplied to it, how it uses eyes, nose and mouth in selecting what it will enjoy.

This peculiar view of the human organism would no doubt irritate the thorough-going rationalist. Groddeck never stopped to consider the objections which could be raised, and which would be worth our considering, since they illustrate very clearly the mechanist-vitalist controversy which lies at the basis of all speculation. What would a critic say? Something, perhaps, along the following lines:

'That a case of inoperable cancer might be made to yield to psycho-analysis and massage is well within the bounds of belief. Freud has already broached the boundaries between the conscious and unconscious intentions of the psyche. I accept that perfectly well. But if a thousand people contract typhoid from a consignment of fruit are we to assume that the individual It of each and every one of them has chosen this form of self-expression in a desire for self-punishment?' It is a tricky question, and Groddeck never set himself to answer it. But if you accept his metaphysical view of things there is no reason why his It-hypothesis should not be given a wide enough applica-

tion to cover even an idea as crazy as this must seem. He
might well have replied that just as the single cell has its
It-ego polarity, and the whole individual his, so also could
any body or community develop its own. You raise your
eyebrows? The conventions of the logic by which we live
demand that while we credit the individual with his own
unique individuality we deny such a thing to concepts like
'state', 'community' and 'nation'—concepts which we use
daily as linguistic counters. When our newspapers speak
of a 'community wiped out by plague' or of a 'nation
convulsed by hysteria' we accept the metaphor easily
enough, though our consciousness rejects those formations
as fictions. Why? In time of war a nation is treated as an
individual with certain specified characteristics. *The Times*
reports on the health 'of the Nation', politicians 'go to the
Country'. This unity we consider a fiction—yet could it
not reflect, in its component parts, the shadow of an individual unity which, is, according to Groddeck, no less a
fiction—man as an ego? If a national ego why not a
national It?

I see you remain unconvinced. So do I. What, you are
perhaps thinking, of the domain of pure misadventure—a
man hurt by a falling wall, the victim of a train-crash?
Are we to blame the patient's It? Well, we know next to
nothing about predisposition—it is a term much used in
science to cover cases where the links of causality appear
obvious, where effects follow clearly from a cause; thus a
victim of hereditary syphilis satisfies the syntax of our
logic, while the victim of a train-crash seems simply the
passive object of fate. . . Yet the truth is that all relations
between events and objects in this world partake of the
mystery of the unknown, and I doubt if we are more
justified in covering one set of events with concepts like
'disease' or 'illness', and leaving others to be entered
against such terms as 'accident' or 'coincidence'. Those
who use words should be careful not to put themselves at

the mercy of words. Groddeck's methods of exposition
indicate how wily a metaphysician he is in this respect.

I should tell you something about the onset of diseases but
the truth is that on this subject I know nothing. And about
their cure. . . . Of that, too, I know just nothing at all. I take
both of them as given facts. At the utmost I can say something about the treatment and that I will do now. The aim
of the treatment, of all medical treatment, is to gain some influence over the It. . . . Generally speaking people have been
content with the method called 'symptomatic treatment' because it deals with the phenomena of diseases, the symptoms.
. . . We physicians look around for a cause and first theoreti-
cally establish . . . that there are apparently two essentially
different causes, an inner one, *causa interna*, which man con-
tributes of himself, and an outer one, *causa externa*, which
springs from his environment. And accepting this clear distinction we have thrown ourselves . . . upon the external
causes, such as bacilli, chills, over-heating. . . . Nevertheless
in every age there have always been physicians who raised
their voices to declare that man himself produced his
diseases, that in him are to be found the *causae internae*. . . .
There I have my jumping-off point. . . . The new thing is the
point of attack in the treatment, the symptom which appears
to me to be there in all circumstances, the 'I'.

But all this is only to demonstrate to you how far we are
from the mechanist view of things, how far we have
travelled from the formalized frontiers of Freud's system.
I am not concerned with your belief or disbelief in Groddeck's hypothesis. I am concerned to show that so-called
rational methods have finally led us to dethrone the 'ego',
to seek in it the source of our malorientation to the world
of reality—the unknown It outside. This is worth observ-
ing if we are to get any purchase on the later development
of poetry, on its orientation towards a more mystical view
of things. It should also give us a clue about the latest
writings of Aldous Huxley and Somerset Maugham, two
novelists who are actively engaged in the propaganda of

non-attachment, as the Buddhists call the new reality. Time and the ego are the two centres of focus for all contemporary poets with any pretensions to message. You will find this wherever you look, in the work of Auden and Spender, no less than in the recent work of Eliot or Edith Sitwell.

Now while it is true that the Christian religion claims to transcend personality, this is an aspect of things which has been lost sight of. It is being revived as an idea through the sacred books of the East which gives it an unfamiliar, and often irritating appearance. We of this age have arrived at this point, you must not forget, with the help of the rationalist science of fact and experiment—a curious journey.

> The power of the eye to see depends entirely on power of the vision inherent in that Light which sees through the eye but which the eye does not see; which hears through the ear, but which the ear does not hear; which thinks through the mind but which the mind does not think. It is the unseen Seer, the unheard Hearer, the unthought Thinker. Other than It there is no seer, hearer, thinker.

These words of *Shri Khrishna Prem* seem to be as applicable to Western metaphysics today as to Eastern.

Groddeck's ego-It polarity is a brilliant rationalization of the Eastern mystic's position—who seeks to free himself from the opposites of being, and to emerge into Reality. It is also in a rough sort of way the key to the contemporary situation in art, whether you read a Christian poet like Eliot or Kathleen Raine, or whether you turn to the writings of Gerald Heard and Huxley. The keynote is reintegration and acceptance of the warring opposites.

> Every observation, (says Groddeck), is necessarily one-sided, every opinion a falsification. The act of observing disintegrates a whole into different fields of observation, whilst in

order to arrive at an opinion one must first dissect a whole
and then disregard certain parts. . . . At the present time we
are trying to recover the earlier conception of a unit, a body-
mind, and make it the foundation of our theory and action.
. . . We understand man better when we see the whole in
each of his parts, and we get nearer to a conception of the
universe when we look upon him as part of a whole.

To speak of reality at all is to limit and debase it; in
understanding poetry it is always the words which get in
the way. It is a great pity that we cannot inhale poems like
scents—for crude as their medium is, their message, their
content is something which owes little to reason. That is
why one should, if possible, allow poems to impact themselves upon one without too much dissection of detail. Let
them be totals to experience first of all; then afterwards see
if your brains and your reading cannot add to the first
impression and support it. The great enemy is the conceptual syntax and the dictionary meanings. Yet used
properly to supplement experience they can become great
allies.

The question of Time is no less important. You should
let the whole poem flow through you as a cinema film
flows across your vision. You should be receptive in the
way that you are when you see an exciting film. You do
not think too consciously about it, you let the successive
scenes flash upon you, surprising you. In a moment they
are gone, yet your attention is busy with the new image on
the screen. Only when the film or the poem has ended
should you begin to think about it and call up your powers
of judgment. But while you are experiencing it you should
be receptive—nothing more. Do not blunt its impact by
too much head-work.

The gap between science, art and religion, then, is
narrowing very considerably. Space-time is still only a
dead mental hypothesis which has, so to speak, not been
allowed to escape from its equations into reality. But if we

are to think about birth and death under the new terms, as expressed in the poetry of our contemporaries, we might find ourselves agreeing with Apollonius of Tyana, who says:

> There is no death of anyone, but only in appearance, even as there is no birth of any, save only in seeming. The change from being to becoming seems to be birth, and the change from becoming to being seems to be death, but in reality no one is ever born, nor does one ever die. It is simply a being visible and then invisible . . . whole becomes parts and parts become whole in the one-ness of the all. . . . And what other name can we give to it but primal being? 'Tis it alone that acts and suffers, becoming all for all through all, eternal deity, deprived and wronged of its own self by names and forms.

For him also past, present and future have suddenly focused themselves properly—have become an Is. Is this not what Professor Whitehead means when he says:

> The present bears in its own realized constitution relationships to a future beyond itself. Cut away the future and the present collapses, emptied of its proper content. Immediate existence requires the insertion of the future in the crannies of the present.

We are moving towards a new metaphysics—at any rate new for us. It is, of course, no older than Pythagoras, while only our lack of knowledge about China prevents us from studying Lao Tzu's sources. In a recent anthology Aldous Huxley tries to show that non-attachment is the philosophic basis of all religions, and that all mystics agree about it. If you look at the book honestly and carefully, without sectarian prejudice, I think you will be forced to agree. 'The Perennial Philosophy' stretches like a bridge between Lao Tzu and St. John of the Cross, between Eliot and Rilke, between Auden and John Donne.

We have travelled a long way in too short a time. I can only hope this brief survey of thought in the last hundred years serves its purpose, though it cannot be considered anything like exhaustive. If I have succeeded in showing you relevant relationships between ideas and the arts I shall consider that the real heavy work is over. Once we have established the angle of fire the poetry of today or yesterday does not seem such a formidable target. Once you have the key to the contemporary situation it should be easy to show you over the whole house. But the historical method, against which I warned you, will have already demonstrated its limitations. We can lay down trends and developments, 'curves' and 'straight lines', but of course they are never completely accurate.

In the historical curve we have followed out you can see the gradual abdication of the absolute rationalist before the growing consciousness of a new reality. Reason has failed us—but only because we expected more than it could give. The idea of wisdom is replacing the idea of knowledge—though to look at our materialistic world, our technocratic civilization, you would hardly think so. Nevertheless the current has set away from scientific rationalism of the old sort.

This brings us to another aspect of affairs worth a moment's thought. The new logic, borrowed from cosmology and expressed in poetry, yields one an original and often bewildering syntactical scheme. It is as if the order has been reversed by the poet in order to show how at home he is in the new extra-logical universe, where causality and time are no longer certain certainties.

Lewis Carroll, writing to a little girl, says:

'I like very much a little mustard with a bit of beef spread evenly under it; and I like brown sugar—only it should have some apple-pudding mixed with it to keep it from being too sweet. I also like pins, only they should always have a cushion put round them to keep them warm. And I like two or three handfuls of hair, only they should always have a little girl's head beneath them to grow on, or else, whenever you open the door, they get blown all over the room and then they get lost, you know.

This detachment of the object from its frame of reference, which afterwards (these words were written in 1876) became an article of faith with the surréalists, has the effect of restoring the mystery innate in the object to which habit has dulled us, and association blunted our responses. Much of this reverse-order technique you will find in modern poetry today. It reflects our awareness of the new Time.

Now, we have traced the gradual subjective curve taken by poetry and prose during the past hundred years. The drama which used to be precipitated outside, became the personal drama of the artist's life—hence the interest in his biography. The artist became an autist (to borrow a word from psychology which is derived from 'autos' meaning 'self'), he became a Selfist.

If we follow the curve through until we come to our own times we see that yet another change has come about, in the wake of the balance and harmony which seem to be the artist's objectives today. He has become aware of the necessity to transcend personality—and he is indicating clearly enough that this is a solution for which the Western civilization to which he belongs is more than ready.

The poetry of the moment is deeply moralistic in implication. The artist has turned his eyes away from art and appears to be studying for a new rôle—that of saint.

It may sound odd at first, but a brief reading of the latest Auden and Eliot should confirm this statement. In both we may see a desire to express the idea of personality transcended—and since the art of the West is based upon

87

personality we might do well to ask ourselves what sort of art is likely to emerge in the future. Will the pendulum swing back again and give us a new art, a genuinely cathartic, exteriorized art, where the new ideas will be, not the subject-matter for tractarianism (as in Huxley), but a kind of underlying implication—a new foundation? Or is art finished for the West? I mean, of course, art as we know it?

This is a problem serious enough to merit some attention. Let me quote from Otto Rank's *Art and Artist*—the only book I have seen to date which faces the question squarely and attempts to elucidate it after examining all the relevant material gathered by sociology, history, psycho-analysis and æsthetics:

Now, however, this last function of art having worked itself out as far as is psychologically possible, the problem of the individual is to put his creative force directly into the service of this formation of personality, without the assistance of art. The more an individual is driven towards real life the less will traditional art-forms help him—indeed they have, for the most part, been already shattered individualistically. Especially in poetry which of course represents in general this conscious level of artistic creation, this permeation by the personal psychology of the poet and the psychological ideology of our age is almost completed. Even the last element of art which poetry retains, language, is becoming more and more an echo of realistic talk or a psychological expression of intellectual thought. . . . But the reality which modern art seeks to reproduce cannot be represented in language, and other traditional forms are suited only to the creative form of the spiritual and not to a realistic expression of the actual. . . .

The new type of humanity will only become possible when we have passed beyond this psychotherapeutic transitional stage, and must grow out of those artists themselves who have achieved a renunciant attitude towards artistic production. A man with creative power who can give up artistic expression in favour of the formation of personality—

since he can no longer use art as an expression of an already developed personality—will remould the self-creative type and be able to put his creative impulse *directly* in the service of his own personality. . . .

You will see from this quotation how much the objectives of the artist have changed since Rimbaud set himself a deliberate and reasoned disorientation of all the senses. . . . There is no doubt that for the West until now the artist has been forced to purchase his art at the cost of his life—his ordinary living. Is it possible that the modern artist will find other uses for his talents of soul? Contemporary poetry with its deep interest in metaphysics certainly argues a change along these lines. If, as Otto Rank suggests, we are in a transitional stage, and the artist is becoming a new kind of person—a seer—what is to become of art?

The artistic individual has lived in art-creation instead of actual life, letting his work live or die on its own account, and has never wholly surrendered himself to life. In place of his own self the artist puts his objectified ego into his work, but though he does not save his subjective mortal ego from death, he yet withdraws himself from real life. And the creative type who can renounce this protection by arts and can devote his whole creative force to life and the formation of life will be the first representative of the new human type, and in return for this renunciation will enjoy, in personality-creation and expression, a greater happiness.

These, then, are some of the issues which face the artist; but they also face us if we are to interpret the artist and let him enrich our own living—which is one of the functions of art in all ages. If he has changed his objectives, we shall soon have to change ours or forfeit the value of the kind of message that he has to give us.

It is at this point that I should like to bring this brief sketch of the artist's preoccupations to a close. I am fully aware that it is inadequate and that its brevity has caused me to take serious liberties with my material. That cannot be helped. The main lines of attack are there, and can be followed up at leisure through the jungles of physics, anthropology and science. As for poetry: in the last analysis great poetry reflects an unknown in the interpretation and understanding of which all knowledge is refunded into ignorance. It points towards a Something which itself subsists without distinction. In this sense, then, art is useless, though in others it has its definite uses. A good poem is a congeries of symbols which transfers an enigmatic knowledge to the reader. At its lowest power you can find the faculty in the nickname or the nursery rhyme: at its highest it reflects a metaphysical reality about ourselves and the world. Thinking about it is useful provided one is thinking for thought's sake or the poem's. It should not be made a topic for degrees and theses. And above all one should never forget that poetry, like life, is altogether too serious not to be taken lightly.

## CHAPTER 5

## POETRY IN THE NINETIES

THE year 1890 makes a convenient point of departure for the student of modern writing in general—and the student of modern poetry in particular. It marks the twilight age of the greater Victorian poets. Browning died in 1889 and while Tennyson, Ruskin and Pater were still alive and producing, their influence was beginning to show a gradual decline upon the graph. Swinburne and William Morris were firmly established but had little more to add to the work which had brought them their well-deserved reputations. New voices were beginning to be heard and new movements to stir below the placid surface of Victorian life. A critic of tendencies, faced with dissimilar and overlapping talents, might discern three types of influence at work in this period.

Among those whose choice of subject-matter and attitude indicated a lively belief in the Empire and all it stood for, side by side with a conviction that the English *mystique* was built upon chivalry and a taste for adventure, he might list the names of Kipling, Henley, Watson and Newbolt. These were the poets of the white man's burden and Imperial Preference. They were not, of course, exactly contemporaneous from the chronological point of view. The second group might be labelled 'Symbolists and Decadents'. It would include the names of Oscar Wilde, Arthur Symons, Ernest Dowson, and it drew much of its intellectual nourishment from the French schools. The third section—that of the 'Ironists', would be headed by the name of A. E. Housman and would most probably include Thomas Hardy.

Of the first group mentioned Kipling is in many ways the most interesting, and in other ways the most baffling, of poets. Certainly his name would rank high on the list of those writers who have endured grave critical injustice because the main ideas which animate his work have fallen into disfavour with a generation that looks chiefly to the London School of Economics for its spiritual nourishment. Kipling saw himself as an old-fashioned tribal bard and much of his poetry represents the 'muscular Christianity and spiritual uplift' of the mid-Victorian period.

As a colonial he was inclined to be more English than the English themselves; as a widely travelled man he had been able to grasp at first hand the sheer geographical magnitude of the Empire and the problems which faced us as a nation if we were to fulfil our function as the representatives of magnanimity and order set up (it seemed) by God over 'lesser breeds without the law'. There was little modesty about this attitude and certainly as little room for self-criticism; but it would be equally true to say that the virtues and attitudes which Kipling extolled were, in their own kind, deserving ones. There is a magnificent barbarism about the Victorian period which reminds one of the age of Elizabeth; a certainty and directness of principle which was touching and uplifting. There was also, of course, an element of self-deception, of hypocrisy: and these latter factors constituted the target-area of two generations of Fabian critics—dramatists like Bernard Shaw, for example—and of those Georgians whose sensibilities had been wounded by the horrors of the first world war. In fact the stock Victorian attitude, or what it was conceived to be, was pilloried consistently up to the 1930's—personified in the middle class bourgeois. But for Kipling England and the Empire were symbols which enjoyed a complete poetic validity unqualified by pious self-questioning and doubts about the social justice of our legislation in various parts of it. Of the general pattern of his working methods the sentiments in the following verse bear witness::

> When 'Omer smote 'is bloomin' lyre,
> E'd 'eard men sing on land and sea;
> An' what 'e thought 'e might require
> 'E went and took the same as me.

He took much of his raw material from the common life and common speech of his day. With an eye already trained to journalism he developed a gift for verse-reportage which, if crude in shape and style, carried the stamp of a curious personal authority: Kipling, as far as one can see, never failed to hypnotize a public. In terms of audience-reaction he was successful with everything he turned his hand to, whether prose or verse. Robert Graves, in the course of a bitterly satiric essay in irritation which professes to be criticism, writes:

At the same time that Kipling gave the Anglo-Indian administrator his *Deuteronomy*, he also gave the English private soldier in India his: in *Soldiers Three* and *Barrack Room Ballads*. This was another benefit, because British Grenadier sentiment was not consonant with the popular Victorian view of the common soldier as a lost soul badged for Hell by the very red of his coat, a view which was also held by the Anglo-Indians of superior rank. . . . The soldier accepted this practical code; or rather his Kipling-reading officers accepted it for him, as his godfathers; and so from 1887 until 1914 all time-serving soldiers grew more and more to be Kipling's Own—to a fantastic degree in the more imaginative cases. . . . Later, Kipling made the Merchant Service literary in much the same way, and gave it absolution in much the same terms. Later still, the Royal Navy, though conservative in religious matters, was not averse from submitting to the Kipling spell. The only two conditions which the sailors made were that he should be technically accurate in his writing and remember their religious sensibilities: these conditions he observed.

The whole of the essay from which I quote is written in the same vein, and is a brilliant example of the way in which Kipling succeeded in disgusting and infuriating the generation which followed him: a generation whose disillusion flowered on the battlefields of the first world war. It is unfair, in a sense, because it does not mention that Kipling is a successful public myth-maker, whose poetry contains a distinctly mysterious quality. When one has subtracted the vulgarity, the crudeness of his political beliefs, and everything else which might seem distasteful to one today, it nevertheless remains true that there are qualities left which simply cannot be wished away or jeered impatiently out of existence. What are they?

Kipling had a gift to exploit which only major poets have—a gift for lodging his phrases in the nervous system, so to speak, in the memory. Many of his lines went straight into the common speech of the British people, and have stayed there. This gift is one which he shares with the greatest poets, and is quite unanalysable as a quality. It is a mark of the major voice, though one does not on the whole feel Kipling to be a major poet. One can only deplore the fact that he concentrated on drawing portraits of the common emotions of the time, and did not give us more of himself. As a workman he tended to be slipshod, and nothing is more depressing to study than his *Collected Poems*, for they indicate little emotional or technical advance, from first to last. There is a cheap finality about much of his workmanship which one cannot help deploring; one feels that he never advanced after 1900 or so. His bones had set, so to speak. Yet after every critical reservation has been made he still remains a great poet, if not a major one. His ability to strike at the nervous system and achieve his response makes his place secure in literature, however much his 'message' may date.

If we were to take his poem *If* as a subject for study we might observe in it his ability to hit off an emotion

94

with the common touch and at the same time to achieve full emotional impact with what he has to say. The popularity of *If* has staled it for us today. The sentiments it expresses may no longer be fashionable, yet *If* deserves careful study both as a poem and as a sociological document.

Its construction (it is simply a rhymed jingle) is so artless as to be deceptive, yet it has discipline and form. But even more interesting is the sociological angle. If one wanted to study the Jewish peoples' attitude to life in the time of Moses one would, no doubt, begin with the Ten Commandments. The same applies to *If*; it is to the British people what the ten tablets were to the Jews. The poem sums up much that they think they should be—and much that they proudly know they are. It is the code of the Samurai of the British Empire—and if today it seems to us banal or even hypocritical it is not Kipling's fault. He was an accurate painter of emotions. Nor is the poem to blame. It has enjoyed a tremendous circulation. (Indeed, its popularity was such that during my own youth in India no party was considered complete without a public recitation of it: while several hundred thousand copies, engraved in art script upon vellum, hung beside the shaving-mirrors of all right-minded colonials, to enable them to begin the day with a brief reminder of what England expected from them. To us today this might seem laughable, but the fact remains that no one who wished to form an impression of the sentiments and ethics of the average Briton at this time could afford to neglect this succinct and masterly expression of them.) This is how the Englishman of pre-war times saw himself; this is how many Englishmen today still see themselves.

Our distaste for the rawness and banality of *If*, then, comes perhaps from the post-war feeling of guilt, the feeling that we have never managed to live up to the sentiments expressed in it. But as sentiments the recipes

for right-minded detachment expressed in the poem seem
to me to be above reproach; while the promise that if one
carried them out one would be a 'man' is to the last degree
illuminating. By 'man' Kipling, of course, means a 'gentleman'—that mysterious and compelling symbol which
haunts the average Englishman to this day, and is responsible for the way he thinks and dresses—and all too often
the way he talks. Nobody can fully understand the peculiar
structure of the British temperament unless he has an idea
of what this symbol stands for in the unconscious of the
race.

It is of the utmost significance for us to do so, for the
shape of English society has always been, and presumably
always will be, in essence aristocratic, monarchist and
quixotic. However much we may laugh at Kipling's *If*,
there is no doubt that even today the unconscious of the
British race is dominated by the idea underlying it. Everybody wants to be a gentleman in Kipling's sense of the
word; and those who by birth or breeding are not gentlemen pay diligent tribute to the symbol by unconscious
imitation. The ideal is by no means as bad as it might
seem: courage, dignity, unselfishness and so on are excellent ethical objectives whether they lead to the kingdom
of heaven or not. But whether we like it or not we must
accept this ineradicable predisposition towards the code
of the Samurai as part and parcel of the British way of life.
It colours our politics, our civic habits, our social behaviour—and if the truth must be told, nearly every
generous impulse in the field of political development has
come out of this rather irritating predisposition.

Why, then, should we react so violently against *If* today? I think I can guess at the reason. It is that the
essentially 'gentle' qualities implied in the word 'gentleman' have changed their shape and assumed a revolting
bourgeois form. 'Gentleness' has given place to 'gentility'
as a form of codified behaviour which no longer comes

from a spiritual attitude so much as from a gross and banal prejudice. Perhaps Kipling is to blame for having made explicit a code of behaviour which was all very well as an unconscious factor in British psychology, but which today is being travestied by the false gentility and the gross superiority complex of the middle classes and the colonial elements of the Empire. But Kipling only portrayed what he saw. Perhaps the rise of the industrial middle classes is really to blame. For the age in which he wrote was an age of gradual decline in aristocratic social values; in some ways it copied the later Elizabethan age, with its squamous new middle class, its 'carpet knights'. Queen Victoria celebrated her two jubilees in 1887 and 1897.

The first British Socialist organization of any note was founded in 1881, with William Morris as one of its chief supporters. The Fabian Society, which was to attract all the young Socialist talents of the age, was formed in 1883 . . . While the sentiments of imperialism and patriotism were in the ascendant they had passed their meridian. The reaction was just beginning. The Boer War and the Great War were the final determinant of the poetic attitude which Kipling expressed so well for the middle classes of the nineties. I say 'middle classes' advisedly, for even Kipling at times grew despondent and irritated by the torpor and unimaginative sloth of the 'gentleman'; his bitter references to 'the flannelled fools at the wicket' and 'the muddied oafs at the goal' betray his impatience with the mental sluggishness of the public school boy, his refusal to become a good empire-builder. It is an essentially middle-class irritation against social pretensions and studied irresponsibility; an irritation which was expressed again in the thirties by the 'New Signatures Group.'

But in Kipling the sentimental imperialist found a voice and a facile (perhaps all too facile) self-justification for his attitude to life. But if Kipling was the self-appointed laureate of the Empire, his attitude, though not his mannerism, found a ready echo in W. E. Henley, who was also a journalist and romantic. Henley has left us a few good poems, but he is more interesting as a forerunner of the Georgians. He experimented with free verse, and with different types of stanza, and at his best achieved remarkable effects.

> For earth and sky and air
> Are golden everywhere,
> And golden with a gold so suave and fine
> The looking on it lifts the heart like wine.
> Trafalgar Square
> (The fountains volleying golden glaze)
> Shines like an angel-market. High aloft
> Over his couchant Lions, in a haze
> Shimmering and bland and soft,
> A dust of chrysoprase,
> Our Sailor takes the golden gaze
> Of the saluting sun, and flames superb,
> As once he flamed it on his ocean round. . . .
>
> The Golden City! And when a girl goes by,
> Look as she turns her glancing head,
> A call of gold is floated from her ear;
> Golden, all golden! In a golden glory,
> Long lapsing down a golden coasted sky,
> The day, not dies, but seems
> Dispersed in wafts and drifts of gold, and shed
> Upon a past of golden song and story
> And memories of gold and golden dreams.

The prescription is a rich and heady one: patriotism, romance, and too many images seem to be the main ingredients. Yet the writing, though rather too juicy, is good. The tradition, too, was a popular one, and did not suffer from lack of imitators. If time and circumstance appear to have staled much of the work of this period we must still admire these poets and their work, and accord them a reasonably high place in the literary tradition of England.

In this context we should mention the work of Sir Henry Newbolt and Alfred Noyes, whose verses were distinguished by fluency and popular patriotism; their work leads on towards the Great War and the abrupt reaction which followed it. We may consider Masefield's poems of adventure in far countries, and the patriotic exclamations of Brooke and Julian Grenfell as following out this masculine tradition which only the bitter experience of war, and the post-war reaction, were to qualify.

What of the 'Decadents'? They belonged to a more artificial and more highly coloured tradition. A convenient point of focus for a study of their attitudes and achievements would seem to be the 'Yellow Book' of 1894 which enshrined much of the talents of these latter-day Symbolists. Oscar Wilde, Aubrey Beardsley, Sir Max Beerbohm, Baron Corvo, Arthur Symons were responsible for the drift of the prevailing winds, which seemed to have set in a westerly direction—away from machinery and utilitarian preoccupations, away from guild socialism and imperialism, and towards the islands of Disenchantment whose position on the charts had been first recorded by Baudelaire—the grandfather of the French Symbolists. To a great extent the whole of this empurpled tradition owed its orientation to the French. The lilies and languors were imported, not home-grown. Swinburne had provided a rough working model in style; Baudelaire, Gérard de Nerval, Verlaine, suggested that the quarries of sensation and artifice were still full of treasures for those who cared to dig hard enough. More important still was Baudelaire's working credo of 'dandyism', which so fascinated Wilde. 'The future,' wrote Wilde, 'belongs to the dandy. It is the exquisites who are going to rule.'

But if Baudelaire was the father of French symbolism

some distinction should be made between his work and that of his step-children. For Baudelaire poetry was still a means of direct communication. He was interested in style. To a certain extent both Verlaine, Gautier and others of this group shared his classical predisposition. They were revolutionary more for choice of subject-matter than for style. The symbolist of the second type, however, the Rimbaud, Laforgue, Isidore Ducasse, was altogether a different person; his work is semantically disturbed. It jumps the points at every curve. He is trying to render states of mind in words—not to communicate according to the accepted laws of common syntax. The common factor in both may be imagery and subject-matter; but there is a huge gap between the intentions of one and the intentions of the other.

The point is worth stressing because the Decadents of the nineties owed all their material and much of their emotional attitude to the poets of the first category, while the influence of Laforgue and Rimbaud did not make any impact on English literature before 1910 or thereabouts. The poets of 'The Yellow Book' found the guilt and hysteria of Baudelaire and Huymans quite enough to be going on with; most important of all, they were glad to accept the canons of 'dandyism' as an axis of behaviour: if they were decadent they were determined to be decadent in a gentlemanly way. Part of their revolt was, after all, directed against the dreary values of middle-class industrialism. They were against the middle classes and spent a good part of their time and energy in astonishing them; but they were also determined advocates of style and elegance. The search for the perfect phrase, however—a treasure-hunt first instituted by Walter Pater whose *Marius the Epicurean* exercised a decisive influence over the period —often led to the ridiculous rather than the sublime. This is Oscar Wilde:

Your eyes are like fantastic moons that shiver in
    some stagnant lake,
Your tongue is like some scarlet snake that dances
    to fantastic tunes,
Your pulse makes poisonous melodies, and your
    black throat is like the hole
Left by some torch or burning coal on Saracenic
    tapestries.

There was much in the work of the Decadents which
made it seem a very tepid and watered-down version of its
French original. There was hardly a flesh-and-blood
negress anywhere. There were plenty of worm-eaten
corpses and blood-flecked lilies, plenty of hysteria and
attitudinizing—but for the most part the poetry of the
nineties rings hollow today. The truth is perhaps that the
English poet tends to suffer from a deficit of sexual and
emotional experience. His life is not raw enough. He is
sealed up among the prohibitions and anxieties of a
puritan culture and this makes it difficult for him to react
to real experience. Baudelaire's subject-matter, despite its
garish presentation, is always real experience, real
anxiety. His writing connects with his life at all points,
while his dandyism is a genuine expression of both. But the
poet of the nineties nearly always seems to be faking up his
subject-matter. Instead of absinthe and negresses, we feel
that he has been writing from a more limited range of
experience: moonshine, barmaids, and soda-water. Nevertheless much that he did was fine. Oscar Wilde, for
example, who hid his greatness under a talent for dinner-
table conversation, left us, in his *Ballad of Reading Gaol*
one of the great ballads in the language; there are not
many poems of the period which will stand comparison
with it. In general however the nineties produced unsatis-
fying work. The despair expressed in most of the poetry of
these dandies seems thin and precious beside that of
Baudelaire. Their emotions seem to have had a very low

melting-point. Nevertheless there were real poets among them.

Pure poetry and the cult of Walter Pater were also the ideals behind the foundation of *The Rhymers' Club* in 1891. Foundation members of this group included W. B. Yeats, Ernest Dowson, Lionel Johnson, and Arthur Symons. They combined Paterism and dandyism in equal parts. They burned with a hard gem-like flame. Despite their archness and over-sophistication they suffered a number of casualties. Some went mad, while others took refuge in the Church. It was an age of ample gestures. Even those who based their work more on Pater than on Baudelaire felt obliged to subscribe to the latter's dandyism in their lives. Their subject matter, which showed a predilection for green absinthe and prostitutes, gave great offence to the common reader. Yet some of it was good:

> Her cheeks are hot, her cheeks are white;
> The white girl hardly breathes tonight,
> So faint the pulses come and go,
> That waken to a smouldering glow
> The morbid faintness of her white.
>
> What drowsing heats of sense, desire,
> Longing and languorous, the fire
> Of what white ashes, subtly mesh
> The fascination of her flesh
> Into a breathing web of fire?
>
> Only her eyes, only her mouth,
> Live, in the agony of drouth,
> Athirst for that which may not be;
> The desert of virginity
> Aches in the hotness of her mouth. . . .

Arthur Symons, who wrote the above lines, has a double claim upon our attention, for he was the first critic of Symbolism, and its first interpreter to English poets. His *The Symbolist Movement in Literature* (1899) exercised a great influence upon many poets of the period. Much of the intentions and some of the practice of these poets may seem suspect, but there is no doubt that at their best they produced memorable work. Even the least of them produced one good poem. We might choose Ernest Dowson's *Non sum qualis eram bonae sub regno Cynarae* as one excellent example of the merits and defects of the prevailing style.

> All night upon mine heart I felt her warm heart beat,
> Night-long within mine arms in love and sleep she lay;
> Surely the kisses of her bought red mouth were sweet;
> But I was desolate and sick of an old passion,
>     When I awoke and found the dawn was gray:
> I have been faithful to thee, Cynara! in my fashion.
>
> I have forgot much, Cynara! gone with the wind,
> Flung roses, roses riotously with the throng,
> Dancing, to put thy pale, lost lilies out of mind;
> But I was desolate and sick of an old passion,
>     Yea, all the time, because the dance was long:
> I have been faithful to thee, Cynara! in my fashion.

The poem is a very successful romantic essay, written with a wonderful feeling for musical effects and altered rhythms. If it does not seem completely moving to us it is perhaps that somewhere we detect a hollowness in the tone—the hollowness of inexperience. But this is a defect which another fifty years may well remedy for our grandchildren. Time has a way of coating good poems with quicksilver, and blinding one to their defects of emotional content which might be apparent to the poet's contemporaries. At a distance of half a century this famous anthology-piece may well take its place in the index of famous poems, as a delightful example from a poor period. By that time it will have been separated from its historical context and will be living a life of its own—if it has a life to live. We are still too near to judge it.

We are in the trough of a reaction which has swallowed up the facile and generous emotionalism of the nineties no less completely than it has swallowed Yeats' famous *Lake Isle of Innisfree* which was a stock anthology-piece for some thirty years. This is another product of the period which we should not overlook though it was written rather later. As a poem it does not compare in authority and finish to his last poems, which are some of the purest in the language, but it gives one a picture of the romantic yearnings which beset the poets of the nineties: yearning for a quiet place in some remote country, far from machinery and decadence alike: yearnings common enough to most poets and most periods perhaps. Coleridge and D. H. Lawrence both made plans in their lifetime to get away from modern civilization, and to found a colony of noble souls in some remote part of America. My goodness, who can blame them?

In his autobiography Yeats claims that Huxley and Tyndall deprived him of the 'simple-minded religion' of his childhood, and that he was forced to construct his own religion—'a new religion, almost an infallible church, of poetic tradition'. Shelley and Blake appear to have provided the scriptures for this new and personal religion. But he was to come under many influences at this period. We have mentioned the French Symbolists: Arthur Symons' great critical work on them is dedicated to Yeats, whom he describes as a poet groping towards that mystical acceptance of reality which has always been the lot of Irish poets.

In 1875 theosophy had been founded by Madame Blavatsky. This was a fusion of oriental mysticism and occultism which at once appealed to Yeats' emotional and romantic nature. It offered spiritual objectives more ambitious than the religion of the day could do—release from the cycle of birth and rebirth; it also offered a reinterpretation of the scriptures of the West which linked them up to gnosticism and neo-platonism, and so to the teachings of the East. It is difficult to know how much of a theosophist Yeats was—but the new ideas were so rich in symbolic material that one can realize easily enough how seductive they must have seemed to a young poet.

In 1885 he read A. P. Sinnett's *Esoteric Buddhism* with profound interest, and set about founding a Hermetic Society in Dublin which in 1886 became the Dublin Lodge of the Theosophical Society. It was here that he read Madame Blavatsky's two great books of esoteric lore— *Isis Unveiled* (1877) and *The Secret Doctrine* (1888). Yeats found theosophy rich in esoteric symbolism, and he was not the only poet to do so; but he was perhaps the earliest poet of this generation to turn the language of theosophy to practical use in his poetry. The relevant facts about the movement are worth noting because, though theosophy seemed for some time to go underground—driven there perhaps by the ridicule of the rationalists—it has re-emerged upon the literary scene in the late forties and might be said to have established itself strongly in the foreground of contemporary belief. It offered Yeats a refuge from the men of science, whose barren materialism seemed to be crushing all the meaning out of life; it also provided a useful counter-balance to the excessive self-indulgence of the ordinary symbolists. It was a question of a rose by any other name smelling twice as sweet. Until now Yeats had been using symbolist technique to record sensation and emotion; now he saw that his symbols could also be made to yield esoteric meanings. This was something his temperament very much needed as a counter-balance to his Irish romanticism and fluency. Poetry became something more than beautifully recorded sensation.

In 1887 he joined the London Rosicrucian Society which was known as the The Order of the Golden Dawn, and his thinking began to receive nourishment from the cabalistic and esoteric teachings of Lully, Paracelsus, Agrippa—and other great neglected hermetics. He learnt that the symbol is initiatory and not didactic—and that unless the symbol is linked to a deep subconscious source it does not carry enough weight to pay its way in poetry. Much of this esoteric discipline only came to the surface in his last poetry—where the structure of metaphysical belief has dissolved away, been completely assimilated into his poetic system, to leave the pure shape of song, playing in the air like a fountain. In his last poems the metaphysics is implied by the attitude to reality and not made explicit as a textual commentary.

Of these mystical proccupations as well as of the general condition of poetry, he himself has spoken movingly in *The Symbolism of Poets*:

How can the arts, (he writes), overcome the slow dying of men's hearts that we call the progress of the world, and lay their hands upon men's heart-strings again, without becoming the garment of religion as in old times?

If people were to accept the theory that poetry moves us because of its symbolism, what change should one look for in the manner of our poetry? A return to the way of our fathers, a casting out of descriptions of nature for the sake of nature, of the moral law for the sake of the moral law, a casting out of all anecdotes and of that brooding over scientific opinion that so often extinguished the central flame in Tennyson, and of that vehemence that would make us do or not do certain things; or, in other words, we should come to understand that the beryl-stone was enchanted by our fathers that it might unfold the pictures in its heart, and not to mirror our own excited faces, or the boughs waving outside the window. With this change of substance; this return to imagination, this understanding that the laws of art, which are the hidden laws of the world, can alone bind the imagination, would come a change of style, and we would cast out of serious poetry those energetic rhythms, as of a man running which are the invention of the will with its eyes always on something to be done or undone; and we would seek out those wavering, meditative, organic rhythms, which are the embodiment of the imagination, that neither desires nor hates, because it has done with time, and only wishes to gaze upon some reality, some beauty; nor would it be any longer possible for anybody to deny the importance of form, in all its kinds, for although you can expound an opinion, or describe a thing when your words are not quite well chosen, you cannot give a body to something that moves behind the senses, unless your words are as subtle, as complex, as full of mysterious life, as the body of a flower or of a woman.

Consequently both poetry and theosophy profit by this new integration. But the influence of theosophy was only one of the early influences. In the notes to his *Collected Poems* published in 1933, he writes: 'Many of the poems in *Crossways*, certainly those upon Indian subjects or upon shepherds and fauns, must have been written before I was twenty, for from the moment when I began *The Wanderings of Oisin* (1889), which I did at that age, I believe, my subject-matter became Irish.' No poet of the stature of Yeats has used so much mythological material in his work or so bright a palette without falling into lushness or imprecision. Yet the full extent of his poetic development is quite extraordinary when you consider the periods it covers. In his earliest work, mostly romantic and highly-charged, his style stretched back as far as Tennyson:

> The woods were round them, and the yellow leaves
> Fell like faint meteors in the gloom, and once
> A rabbit old and lame limped down the path;
> Autumn was over him: and now they stood
> On the lone border of the lake once more:
> Turning, he saw that she had thrust dead leaves
> Gathered in silence, dewy as her eyes,
> In bosom and hair.
>
>       'Ah, do not mourn,' he said,
> 'That we are tired, for other loves await us;
> Hate on and love through unrepining hours.
> Before us lies eternity; our souls
> Are love, and a continual farewell.'
>
>                       *(Ephemera,* 1889)

107

The feeling for vowel-sounds and the dreamy and sentimental method of evoking emotion are properties which
remind one at once of Tennyson's *Morte d'Arthur*—whose
swarming mythical cross-currents must have given Yeats
great enjoyment. But even in the same period Yeats
managed to bring off good poems whole without losing
any of the richness of texture: poems which were as much
his own as his latest—though not perhaps as great. Most
of us know verses like:

> The island dreams under the dawn
> And great boughs droop tranquillity;
> The peahens dance on a smooth lawn,
> A parrot sways upon a tree,
> Raging at its own image in an enamelled sea.
>
> Here we will moor our lonely ship
> And wander ever with woven hands,
> Murmuring softly lip to lip,
> Along the grass, along the sands,
> Murmuring how far away are the unquiet lands. . . .
>
> How we  alone of mortals are
> Hid under quiet boughs apart
> While our love grows an Indian star,
> A meteor of the burning heart,
> One with the tide that gleams, the wings that gleam
>     and dart,
>
> The heavy boughs, the burnished dove
> That moans and sighs a hundred days:
> How when we die our shades will rove,
> When eve has hushed the feathered ways,
> With vapoury footsole by the water's drowsy blaze.

There is a little too much of the murmuring, perhaps,
and a hint of weakness in the imprecision of 'how far
away are the unquiet lands', but the poem is saved and

converted by a strong last verse in which 'vapoury foot-sole' and 'burnished dove' are both hard and concise images.

We have spoken of Yeats as a Symbolist and as a theosophist; it remains to record another facet of his protean temperament. Seduced as he was by the methods and attitudes of the Symbolist no less than by the vague and thrilling surmises of the theosophist, Yeats nevertheless always felt himself to be, first and foremost, an Irishman. His poetic equipment at this second stage owed more to Irish folk lore, poetry and myth, than to French or Indian influences. He himself was the first to recognize the fact. With the publication of his *Celtic Twilight* in 1893 came another kind of recognition. The poets of Ireland recognized a master, and it is largely due to Yeats' genius that the Celtic Revival began to shape itself as an articulate idea. . . . In 1898 the Irish Literary Theatre was born and began to produce the poetic plays of the Dublin poets whose acknowledged leader was Yeats.

Of the many and differing talents writing at this time two names deserve our attention—those of Lady Gregory and A.E.—as he chose to pseudonymize himself. The former wrote some interesting poetry but was chiefly famous as a patron and spiritual guide to the Celtic Movement. A.E. had shared Yeats' theosophist leanings, and much of his verse, while it is firmly and beautifully coloured, is altogether too lush to be acceptable. Yet at his best he is a very fine poet.

A.E. was not a great poet as Yeats was: but he shared his absorption in mysticism with many other Irish writers of this epoch. They read the Upanishads and the Rig-Veda, they had visions of eternity, they sat at the feet of Madame Blavatsky and heard the mysteries of Isis revealed to them. This was, of course, the obverse of the medal worn so proudly by the 'Decadents', whose dandyism as a code of behaviour could only offer a watery hedonism to put against their gentlemanly world-weariness. The following passage from *Dorian Gray* expresses this clearly enough:

> '*Fin de siècle*,' murmured Sir Henry.
> '*Fin du globe*,' answered his hostess.
> 'I wish it were *fin du globe*,' said Dorian, with a sigh. 'Life is a great disappointment.'

Nothing could be further from the attitudes of the Celtic revivalists in Dublin, and we must presume that if Yeats and A.E. were ever 'dandies' in the *Yellow Book* sense of the word, they soon turned aside in search of mysticism and hermetic truth. They were lucky in their strong feeling for Irish myth. It centred their poetry upon their own tongue and literature, so that they were spared the perils of a domination by Indian symbolism. The reader who bothers to glance through the pages of *Isis Unveiled* will see clearly enough the dangers which these Irish poets escaped; in the absence of linguistic equivalents for the cold metaphysical Indian terms, Madame Blavatsky turns on all the lush poetic heat of the nineties tradition, and her book (for all the good sense in it) is an orgy of literary imprecision and rhetoric. It was merciful that Yeats and A.E. could relate these Eastern Scriptures to Ireland, and keep their poetic roots deep in the wild soil of their home island. We are the gainers by it.

Of Yeats' later development into the arch-poet of the twentieth century this is not the place to speak. His later work gains when it is laid beside that of Auden and Eliot—for his poetic development was consistent from 1889 until the year of his death.

The case of Hardy is very different; he abandoned the novel, a form which made him famous and by which he is most widely known today, in the nineties, and published his *Wessex Poems* in 1898, which met with a somewhat hostile reception from reviewers who admired his novels. Despite criticism he held his way and published further

collections of verse in 1902 and 1909 which won him a
definite place in the poetic tradition as an ironist—perhaps
even a pessimist, for what the word is worth. Hardy's
poetry is not formally very graceful, but one has the impression in reading it that the rough surface has been
deliberately cultivated in order to avoid sentimentality.
He was anxious perhaps to attempt something a little less
sensuously beautiful than the nature poetry of the day.
From the prison of his old age he recorded his feelings
about nature, about death and love, in a style which, at its
best, is cold and exact and moving. The reviewers of the
1900's thought it a little cruel, as indeed it was; Hardy was
making a faithful picture of his bitterness at approaching
death. Buried in these poems is a faithful reflection of the
amorality of the old, and the poignance with which they
see death daily advancing towards them.

Somewhere in the background of Hardy's work there
is an undertone of despair and scepticism which colours the
whole mood. In his diary he wrote once:

> Perhaps I can express more fully in verse ideas and
> emotions which run counter to the inert crystallized opinion
> —hard as a rock—which the vast body of men have vested
> interests in supporting. To cry out in a passionate poem that
> (for instance) the Supreme Mover or Movers, the Prime
> Force or Forces, must be either limited in power, unknow-
> ing, or cruel—which is obvious enough, and has been for
> centuries—will cause them merely a shake of the head; but
> to put it in argumentative prose will make them sneer, or
> foam, and set all the literary contortionists jumping upon me,
> a harmless agnostic, as if I were a clamorous atheist, which
> in their crass illiteracy they seem to think is the same thing.

If there is any weakness here it comes not out of sentimentality or artifice. Hardy's poetry is clean and exact
—and at the same time touching. One is reminded of
some lines by W. J. Turner which admirably describe the
feeling one has in reading his work:

For the blood of a man when he is old,
Old and full of power,
Is no longer like the blood of a young man, inflammable,
It is like a serpent and an eagle,
A bull violent and immovable,
And a burning that is without flame or substance.
Terrible is the agony of an old man
The agony of incommunicable power
Holding his potency like a rocket that is full of stars
But his countenance is like a sky. . . .

Between 1903 and 1908 came Hardy's most ambitious work, *The Dynasts*. In scope and design this huge dramatic poem was probably the most ambitious work undertaken since Goethe's *Faust*; it is sad to record that it seems to us a failure. The design alone, however, makes it worth reading, even though the quality of the poetry is poor. In *The Dynasts* Hardy has dramatized the chronicle of the Napoleonic Wars, especially as they are related to English affairs. The drama is divided into three parts, comprising nineteen acts, and one hundred and thirty scenes. The best parts of the poem are the prose passages, and the work as a whole is more remarkable for its architectural proportions than for the quality of the work it contains.

A. E. Housman shares little with Hardy beyond a certain stoicism of attitude and dryness of thought. His *A Shropshire Lad* (1896) exercised an enormous influence by the determined severity and cleanness of its execution. It was also new in the sense that it was the work of an ironist published during a period when sentimental melancholy was the vogue.

Therefore, since the world has still
Much good, but much less good than ill,
And while the sun and moon endure
Luck's a chance, but trouble's sure,
I'd face it as a wise man would,
And train for ill and not for good.

The prevailing wind that blows through Housman's verse is a chilly one; irony, scepticism and resignation are the climates it brings. Yet he is a fine poet with his neatly ruled margins and his terse epigrammatic style. His poems always carry tension and power; while the last two lines of each are usually reserved for an irony which comes like a spray of cold water. A much-parodied poet, A. E. Housman is really inimitable when he is at his best; and only his slender output prevents him from securing a higher place in the index of great poets.

Of the other poets who enjoyed a good reputation during this period three deserve mention in passing, Wilfrid Scawen Blunt, Laurence Binyon, and Sir William Watson: while three deserve brief quotation to illustrate their qualities. John Davidson's poetry is sombre; his life was a tragedy. In his passionate love of strength for strength's sake, and in the chilly materialism of his philosophy he might be considered a cousin to W. E. Henley; but his refusal to turn his poetry into a vehicle for sentiment, and his determination to write of common sights and sounds placed him near to the Decadents with their insistence on low-life as a necessary part of poetry's subject matter. But for Davidson the accent lay not on low-life or high-life—but on life as it was, entire, in the round. Though it was an ideal that he could not always live up to his best verse was quite uniquely his own. His poem on the hunting of a stag, for example, contains verse of the finest texture easily and rhythmically knit up in a way which reminds one of Edward Thomas at his best.

> When the pods went pop on the broom, green broom,
> And apples began to be golden-skinn'd,
> We harboured a stag in the Priory coomb,
> And we feather'd his tail up-wind, up-wind,
> We feather'd his tail up-wind—

The death of the stag in the sea is beautifully described:

Three hundred gentlemen, able to ride,
Three hundred horses as gallant and free,
Beheld him escape on the evening tide,
Far out till he sank in the Severn Sea,
Till he sank in the depths of the sea—
The stag, the buoyant stag, the stag
That slept at last in a jewell'd bed
Under the sheltering ocean spread,
The stag, the runnable stag.

Robert Bridges was another poet whose skill and craftsmanship placed him in the front rank of English letters at this period. His reputation was made with his collected *Shorter Poems* published in 1890, which showed delicacy of eye, a real sense of rhythm, and a feeling for observation and description. He is the father of the Georgian Movement which was to be founded in the Cheshire Cheese, a public house which by 1912 was no longer a haunt for Rhymers. Two verses from his poem *Nightingales* will show his qualities.

Beautiful must be the mountains whence ye come,
And bright in the fruitful valleys the streams, wherefrom
    Ye learn your song:
Where are those starry woods? O might I wander there,
Among the flowers, which in that heavenly air
    Bloom the year long!

Nay, barren those mountains and spent the streams:
Our song is the voice of desire, that haunts our dreams,
    A throe of the heart,
Whose pining visions dim, forbidden hopes profound,
No dying cadence nor long sigh can sound,
    For all our art.

Francis Thompson is represented in most anthologies by his *The Hound of Heaven*. It is a poetical *tour de force* which would, had he been able to continue writing at this level, have put him up beside Keats. But unfortunately there is little else of any value in his work, though it is always full of half-achieved effects. He might be described as an 'almost, yet not quite' poet. At his best he is great:

> Naked I wait Thy love's uplifted stroke!
> My harness piece by piece Thou hast hewn from me,
>> And smitten me to my knee;
>> I am defenceless utterly.
>> I slept, methinks, and woke,
> And, slowly gazing, find me stripped in sleep.
> In the rash lustihead of my young powers,
>> I shook the pillaring hours
> And pulled my life upon me; grimed with smears,
> I stand amid the dust o' the mounded years—
> My mangled youth lies dead beneath the heap.

But at his worst he comes near to downright imbecility:

> Little Jesus, wast Thou shy
> Once, and just as small as I?
> And what did it feel like to be
> Out of Heaven and just like me?
> Didst Thou sometimes think of *there*,
> And ask where all the angels were?
> I should think that I would cry
> For my house all made of sky....

When his gifts are measured against his defects, Francis Thompson's failure to write more good poetry must be considered a tragedy of the nineties; he had vision and range and technique enough to equip a major poet, yet he remains a poet of the second rank who brought off one first-rate bit of work.

It should be apparent from the quotations with which we have illustrated the work of these poets that verse-forms were beginning to undergo a transformation. Henley was already playing with free verse, while the long rambling lines of Bridges with their subtle cadences prefigured much that was to come, although genuine metrical innovations affecting syntax did not become apparent much before 1914. Yet a feeling of delight in impressionistic methods is apparent even at this early stage. Masefield's famous anthology piece *Cargoes*, for example, does not (as Robert Graves has long since pointed out) contain a single verb. In the poetry of the thirties even greater compression began to be apparent in the dropping of the article from nouns.

Perhaps this is a good point at which to introduce the names of Henri Bergson and William James: the first is important because of his view on the nature of Time, and the second because he was a forerunner of Freud in a sense. In James' *Principles of Psychology* (1890) there is the famous chapter entitled 'The Stream of Thought' in which he describes how by commencing the 'study of the mind from within' he found 'constant change and a teeming multiplicity of objects and relations'. Consciousness, far from being discrete, proved on introspection to be a continuous flow—a 'stream' or a 'river'. The old stable outlines of the ego were changing, and the novelists were not slow to grasp the fact. We are not one undivided self, they thought, but many selves—in fact a flux of identities without clear and determined outlines. The characters of the novel began, like matter when it was broken down, to radiate not along a series of points but in waves, in wavelets of subjective experience. But if James supplied the artist with that wonderful phrase, 'the stream of consciousness', it was because he was making popular the new idea that psychology was more concerned with processes than with static forms or faculties.

Henri Bergson was also among the great rebels against scientific externality and pure reason. By 'intuition' he had discovered reality to exist in the flux—'the indivisible flux of consciousness' which he called 'Duration'. 'Made

continuous only by memory, which charges each moment
with its past, 'duration' involves a perpetually recurring
present; science, calendars and clocks, claimed Bergson,
had no way of measuring reality, which was Duration.

Since the time of Plato, philosophy had been trying
to get round the idea of Duration by regarding time as an
illusion, and finite being as one with eternity; Bergson
suggested that the very being of which the philosopher
took account when he reflected might be time itself.

He advised writers to throw reason overboard and
depend on 'intuition' which alone was able to capture the
qualities of Duration, which was reality. Reality was not
accessible to reasoning. Thought set up artificial frames
around what was in flux, moving, changing. 'Intuition'
alone could bridge the gap. To a certain extent the work
of novelists like Conrad, Henry James and Joyce—and
also Virginia Woolf—was an extension of these ideas into
the domain of literary form. But where the best of these
artists controlled their material much of the weakness and
silliness of the minor writers sprang from this article of
faith, which had the effect of destroying form. It ruined
Lawrence's novels; Joyce had to borrow his form from
Homer; and much that is tiring in Virginia Woolf comes
from the surrender of a feminine temperament to recorded
sensation. Time and the ego are the two determinants of style
for the twentieth century; if one grasps the ideas about them
one has, I think, the key to much that has happened.

But the surrender to immediate sensation was also an
article of faith with, the nineties—it was part of the
dandyism. In *The Green Carnation* by Robert Hichens,
which is a satire directed against Wilde and dandyism, we
find many passages which express this clearly enough.

'Every sensation is valuable. Sensations are the details
that build up our lives.'

'But if we do not choose our sensations carefully, the

stories may be sad, may even end tragically,' said Lady
Locke.

'O I don't think that matters at all, do you, Mrs.
Windsor?' said Reggie. 'If we choose carefully, we become
deliberate at once; and nothing is so fatal to personality as
deliberation.'

As satire this is accurate enough; but it is also good
Bergson. Of course both James and Bergson were—as
Bergson himself admitted—part of a general movement
towards the acceptance of a new Time, and a new en-
largement of the ego's boundaries. The effect of their ideas,
and later the ideas of Freud and Einstein, may be seen
reflected in the change of forms which the poets and prose-
artists of 1900-1930 brought about.

CHAPTER 6

## GEORGIANS AND IMAGISTS

OSCAR WILDE and Ernest Dowson died in 1900, the one age forty-four, the other thirty-three. Lionel Johnson died in 1902 aged thirty-five. John Davidson committed suicide in 1909, while Francis Thompson died in 1907 aged forty-eight. Those who lived on—and many like Yeats, Bridges, Thomas Hardy and Kipling lived on for twenty or thirty more years of active production—did not receive their full measure of recognition until later. But the era of flowers and fancies ended at the beginning of the century. Dandyism as a code of behaviour ended somewhat earlier—most likely about the time of the prosecution of Oscar Wilde. New names were beginning to be heard. New poets began to occupy the empty seats at the Cheshire Cheese.

In a memoir upon Rupert Brooke, Sir Edward Marsh has described how, in the summer of 1912, the Georgian Movement was launched. The project was discussed at a lunch party in his rooms. Among the poets present were Rupert Brooke, John Drinkwater, W. W. Gibson, Harold Monro and Marsh himself. The idea took public shape in the first Georgian anthology of 1912 which made an immediate impression on the public. Though most of the poets were new, a few established names were to be found in the pages of this and subsequent anthologies. John Masefield was one. The popularity of the Georgian collections continued unabated for a number of years, and the movement might be said to have come to an end somewhere around 1922. But it was something more than just a movement; the intelligence of Harold Monro and

119

the taste of Sir Edward Marsh guided and shaped the course of things.

The Georgian main tradition was bucolic or pastoral. English literature, when it is at a loss for subject matter, always falls back on the sights and sounds of the English country-side, albeit seen through the dense refracting medium of a classical education. Many of the Georgians were pastoral writers, whose vaguely pantheistic attitude to the English scene seemed to make it less dull than one imagines it to have been. Drinkwater, W. H. Davies and (the non-Georgian) Edward Thomas, all did excellent work in this tradition. But there were other poets who also found a place within the hospitable pages of the Georgian anthologies: writers who were soon to go their own way like Aldous Huxley, James Joyce and D. H. Lawrence. Later on many of these writers were to develop along very anti-Georgian lines, but it is a tribute to the taste and sensibility of Harold Monro that he was always ready to print them in his anthologies or issue their first slim volume from his Poetry Bookshop, which for years was the centre of focus for poets in London. In the collection called *Twentieth Century Poetry* the reader will find quite the best introduction to the verse of this period—and perhaps one of the best anthologies ever compiled. Monro's taste was sufficiently elastic to include such differing talents and temperaments as T. S. Eliot, Roy Campbell, Ezra Pound, Edith Sitwell and D. H. Lawrence, side by side with the quieter pastoral writers like Edmund Blunden, W. H. Davies and John Drinkwater. That the Georgians were anxious to establish new verse-forms and were no less anxious to experiment is obvious from the ardour with which they defended free verse—and the ardour with which some of them practised it. But so wide were Monro's tastes that it was impossible to consider that talent so different and so plentiful could ever combine and express a unified attitude to life. The Georgians from their foundation contained all the elements necessary for literary schism and it is not surprising that the tradition should split into groups with the emergence of the Imagists.

The main body of the Georgian tradition proper might be described as Quietist or Pietist. It did not innovate but concentrated on simple musical and pictorial effects. The subject matter was for the best part nature—not 'red in tooth and claw' to be sure: but the simple, humble, day to day events of country-side life. In this tradition (which continues to this day) W. H. Davies, Edward Thomas and John Drinkwater might be considered good craftsmen; this implies no disrespect to Edmund Blunden who was one of these writers, and who holds a firm position in the same tradition to this day. His style developed more slowly, as did that of Walter de La Mare. Yet these verses from a poem, *The Kingfisher* of W. H. Davies give an indication of the central pre-occupations of the Georgian poet, and his technical methods of treating them:

> It was the Rainbow gave thee birth
> And left thee all her lovely hues;
> And, as her mother's name was Tears,
> So runs it in thy blood to choose
> For haunts the lonely pools, and keep
> In company with trees that weep.
>
> Go you and, with such glorious hues,
> Live with proud Peacocks in green parks;
> On lawns as smooth as shining glass,
> Let every feather show its marks;
> Get thee on boughs and clap thy wings
> Before the windows of proud kings.

The general characteristics are all here: the slightly archaic vocabulary—'thou' and 'bosom', the subject-matter, the strict forms and the music of vowel-sounds. This is not, you will be thinking, very far from Robert

Bridges and Hardy. Yet forms, when all is said and done, are modified by temperaments, and the Georgians were for the greater part individual writers still in the process of developing styles suited to their characters. Walter de La Mare, for example, with his command of verbal magic, did nothing very extraordinary from the point of view of technique. Yet his subject-matter, which was so often childhood, and the queer lights he threw over it, marked him early as an individual talent.

## ECHO

'Who called?' I said, and the words
Through the whispering glades,
Hither, thither, baffled the birds—
'Who called? Who called?'

The leafy boughs on high
Hissed in the sun;
The dark air carried my cry
Faintingly on:

Eyes in the green, in the shade,
In the motionless brake,
Voices that said what I said,
For mockery's sake:

'Who cares?' I bawled through my tears;
The wind fell low:
In the silence, 'Who cares? Who cares?'
Wailed to and fro.

Wordsworth might be said to be the great-grandfather of Georgianism, but where Wordsworth heard the terrifying organ-notes of the Christian God echoing everywhere in nature the Georgians felt more at home on the farm. They were content with brief impressionistic sketches of nature, a clear and scholarly enumeration of day to day affairs in the countryside. Their gift was precise observation. They were often sentimental, often weak, and all too often arch. But their best work is part of a very real bucolic tradition in English literature: a tradition which has continued up to today, offering us an unbroken line of nature-poets who have concentrated on simple observations and lucid workmanship.

In this sense both Andrew Young and Richard Church might be classed among these poets today. The temperamental endowment of a nature poet in England is a queer blend of pantheism and pietism; God, for John Drinkwater and for W. W. Gibson, was 'a kindly and friendly figure who probably wore tweeds and smoked a pipe'. He was not a Jehovah. Among the pietists Edmund Blunden, Edward Thomas, contented themselves with localities and atmospheres, but stopped short this side of mysticism. Nature was good enough for them. It is perhaps the limitations of their intentions and predisposition that has made them so often a target for satire. Robert Graves in his essay on Dead Movements has the following criticism to make of them:

> Georgianism was an English dead movement contemporary with Imagism and politically affiliated with the then dominant Liberal party. Although not so highly organized, it had a great vogue between the years 1912 and 1918 and was articulate chiefly upon questions of style. The Georgians' general recommendations were the discarding of archaistic diction such as 'thee' and 'thou' and 'floweret' and 'whene'er' and of poetical constructions such as 'winter drear' and 'host on armed host' and of pomposities generally. It was also understood that, in reaction to Victorianism, their verse should avoid all formally religious, philosophic or improving themes; and all sad, wicked, café-table themes in reaction to the 'nineties. Georgian poetry was to be English but not aggressively imperialistic; pantheistic rather than atheistic; and as simple as a child's

KEY TO MODERN POETRY

reading book. These recommendations resulted in a poetry which could be praised rather for what it was not than for what it was. Eventually Georgianism became principally concerned with Nature and love and leisure and old age and childhood and animals and sleep and similar uncontroversial subjects.


And nigh this toppling reed, still as the dead
   The great pike lies, the murderous patriarch
   Watching the waterpit sheer-shelving dark,
Where through the plash his lithe bright vassals thread.

   The rose-finned roach and bluish bream
   And staring ruffe steal up the stream
   Hard by their glutted tyrant, now
   Still as a sunken bough.

   He on the sandbank lies,
   Sunning himself long hours
   With stony gorgon eyes:
   Westward the hot sun lowers.

Sudden the gray pike changes and quivering poises for
   slaughter;
Intense terror wakens around him, the shoals scud awry,
   but there chances
A chub unsuspecting; the prowling fins quicken, in fury he
   lances;
And the miller that opens the hatch stands amazed at the
   whirl in the water.

            (EDMUND BLUNDEN: *The Pike*)


In this quotation we can see some of the effect of impressionism upon regularity of structure. The poet is letting the ragged lines of his verse not only describe the battle and the commotion in the water, but the poem itself tries to *imitate* the commotion described in its formal properties.

Of the poets of this period none was more highly regarded than Rupert Brooke, whose death during the 1914-1918 war was considered a great loss to letters. In some ways he showed great skill and talent and much of his work is readable today and even moving. But he died too young for us to be sure of his possibilities of development. He is not a great poet as he stands. Perhaps he might have been had he lived through the war. His verse, though thin in subject matter, is free and melodious, and carefully put together.

The Imagists, as they called themselves, were not derivative of the Georgians, though the impulse behind the ideas of Imagism bore fruit at roughly the same time, and poets of either tendency shared the same platform. The impetus originally came from T. E. Hulme, a neo-Bergsonian philosopher and poet (he was also killed in the war) who as early as 1908 founded a club with the intention of restoring the poetry of England. He was joined by two anti-Victorian young men, one of whom was Richard Aldington (now famous as a novelist) and F. S. Flint (a critic much under the influence of French symbolism); while neither of these two were more than minor poets they had drive and critical acumen and were determined not to spare their elders. 'Rhyme and metre', wrote Flint acidly in his *Other World Cadences*, 'rhyme and metre are artificial and external additions to poetry, and that as the various changes that can be rung upon them were worked out, they grew more and more insipid until they have become contemptible and encumbering.'

Later came two Americans, T. S. Eliot and Ezra Pound, bringing with them a new impetus from Montparnasse to shape and guide the movement. The influences under which these poets began were Symbolist, but where the nineties had stuck to Baudelaire and De Nerval, these young men were more interested in Laforgue and Rimbaud. As Imagists they wanted to make a clean break with the rhetoric and subject matter of the Victorians.

They took no interest in the aspects of Baudelaire that had so haunted Wilde. They were after something different—the deliberate violence and dislocations of Baudelaire's step-children. They were very much interested in the possibilities of free verse and they wanted above all to construct poems which would have economy, grace and precision—hitting power. The work of the English contingent looks rather callow today, but the two American poets had something new to offer.

The first Imagist Anthology, edited by Pound, appeared in 1914, but already in 1910 T. S. Eliot had produced his *Portrait of a Lady* and *The Love Song of J. Alfred Prufrock*. In both these poems you can detect a new tone of voice, an irony and deliberation of style which is completely adult.

Once again it appears to be a case of different poetic temperaments making a convenience of a collective name —for while Pound and Eliot share a certain resemblance, nothing could be less like their work than that of the other so-called Imagists. The movement was doomed to perish as all movements will when real poets get in amongst them. But for a time the name Imagism was a convenient point of reference for those poets who felt anti-traditional —Eliot, Pound, and even perhaps D. H. Lawrence. Much of the work of this time was weak and shapeless, but much was good.

In Pound and Eliot a new technique was beginning to shape itself and emerge; Pound's deft pictures were in a class of their own, though his classical leanings and a certain sentimentality of scholarship led him to borrow and copy more than was perhaps necessary for a poet of his very real gifts. Everything was grist to his mill: early Anglo-Saxon, Chinese, Provençal. Eliot's temperament was colder and less given to copying, though his scholarship was deeper and his sensibility wider than that of his compatriot. He was an ironist. Pound seldom rose above his own innate literary idealisms.

In Eliot's poetry of this period we see the poet, not trying to fly from the materialistic age towards scholarship or dandyism, but desperately trying to accommodate the real world within the scheme of his values; and failing. Where other poets fled the real world, or only gave a half-hearted glance or two in its direction, Eliot forced himself not only to look the monster in the face but also to draw its portrait. That the poetry he produced turned out to be a careful ironic portrait of emotional anaemia and spiritual sterility was, strictly speaking, not his fault—it was the fault of the world. Prufrock was no scholar gipsy.

> And indeed there will be time
> For the yellow smoke that slides along the street,
> Rubbing its back upon the window-panes;
> There will be time, there will be time
> To prepare a face to meet the faces that you meet;
> There will be time to murder and create,
> And time for all the works and days of hands
> That lift and drop a question on your plate. . . .

The poem is a moving-staircase of half-uttered associations, memories, questions. Prufrock's portrait is savagely done, yet with a certain coldness of treatment, an irony, a detachment, which we now recognize as part of Eliot's stock in trade. More than this, Prufrock's world—which is our modern world—is brilliantly anatomized: for the first time it plays its part as satirical subject-matter without giving one the feeling that it is inappropriate. It is at once an explanation and a justification of Prufrock's terrible *ennui* in the face of life.

> And indeed there will be time
> To wonder 'Do I dare?' and 'Do I dare?'
> Time to turn back and descend the stair,

With a bald spot in the middle of my hair——
(They will say: 'How his hair is growing thin!')
My morning-coat, my collar mounting firmly to my chin,
My necktie rich and modest, but asserted by a simple pin . . .

The cyclic technique (the problem is stated, but the statement itself is not resolved and ended), the halt and recovery, the perpetual branching off to come back to the argument by another road and from another angle—all these qualities are for the first time successfully deployed into English poetry with complete assurance, complete mastery. And for the first time the modern industrial scene appears to play a legitimate part in the poem. The evening 'spread out against the sky like a patient etherized upon a table', the 'sawdust restaurants with oyster-shells', and the smoke 'that rises from the pipes of lonely men in shirt-sleeves, leaning out of windows' is a clear and lucid picture of the industrial world which Prufrock has inherited. This is, in fact, one of the first poems of city-man. It avoids both escapism and sentimentality. It has a hard metallic flavour of a new style.

In 1914 *The Egoist* was founded, and by this time the break with the main line of Georgian tradition was almost complete. Eliot and Pound had broken the first furrow; they found plenty of support in Aldington and F. S. Flint, who, if they were not particularly good poets, were enthusiastic critics, much influenced by French models.

The weaknesses of the lesser Imagists sprang from an innate English sentimentality and a false sixth-form classicism; Pound's ability saved him from this, though much of his subject-matter and treatment seemed to put him in this category. If we can speak of Eliot's poetry as being 'saved' in this sense, it was because of the diversity of his influences more than anything else. Other and wilder movements were to rise, but none of them held the field for very long. *The Egoist* printed some of the early prose of James Joyce, and some of the brilliant critical polemics of P. Wyndham Lewis—an artist-writer whose paper *Blast* was also launched in 1914 and which devoted itself to a new ism—Vorticism. But the war was rapidly carrying off most of the talented contributors to these papers, and life in the firing-line was not conducive to poetry or prose. There is no doubt that much of the work of this period was extravagant and amusing, and that the Georgians of the quieter kind looked upon these developments as unpleasant, unnecessary, and perhaps downright silly. But both Eliot and Pound were refining their respective styles and trying to eliminate the softness and sentimentality of the earlier Imagist poetry. They wanted to marry dissociation to a firm style. Where other poets interpreted Bergson as an apostle of pure sensation, these two wanted their poems not only to mirror subconscious states, but also to have classical form and cutting-edge. They were perhaps the first poets of this group to rise successfully above self-pity, and to avoid the diffuse and shapeless pantheism which infected so much Georgian verse.

Pound, it is true, replaced sentiment with an exaggerated regard for scholarship in much of his work. His poetry—or much of it—was the work of a classical evangelist; but Eliot's, though encrusted with allusion and direct quotation, was kept very strictly within emotional bounds. It was all gristle. There was very little fat on it. He was the first poet to understand that the true classical tradition could be equated with the latest and most outrageous experimental forms. But it was not until the publication of his *The Waste Land* in 1922 that the turning point might be said to have been reached. Seen at this remove of time there is little to differentiate off the work of the lesser Imagists from the Georgians; the reaction seems to be dependent more on intellectual differences

than on questions of literary principle. Richard Aldington's *Prelude*, for example, is not very different in structure and tone from similar poems constructed in the
Georgian east wing of the mansion of letters. Aldington
writes:

> How could I love you more?
> I would give up
> Even that beauty I have loved too well
> That I might love you better.
> Alas, how poor the gifts that lovers give—
> I can but give you of my flesh and strength,
> I can but give you these few passing days
> And passionate words that since our speech began
> All lovers whisper in all women's ears.

There is no great difference from the technical point of
view between this and J. C. Squire, a minor Georgian,
when he writes:

> Three scattered little trout, as black as tadpoles,
> Came waggling slowly along the glass-dark lake,
> And I swung my arm to drop my pointing worm in,
> And then I stopped again with a little shake.
>
> For I heard the thin, gnat-like voices of the trout
> —My body felt woolly and sick and astray and cold—
> Crying with mockery in them: 'You are not allowed
> To take us, you know, under ten years old.'

It is an artificial inflation of poetic currency, a sentimentality of thought, which unites the two, the Imagist
and the Georgian. In the case of Squire, of course, the
poem ends in the deepest bathos. Aghast at what he is
about to do—to hook trout of less than regulation size—
the poet faints.

And I fainted away, utterly miserable,
Falling in a place where there was nothing to pass,
Knowing all sorrows and the mothers and sisters of sorrows,
And the pain of the darkness before anything ever was.

To separate the War Poets from the main body of the poetry of this period is merely a convenience; much of the best work of Siegfried Sassoon, Robert Graves, Herbert Read, Robert Nichols, had little to do with the war. Yet it was their attitude to the war as subject-matter which di-tinguished them from the other poets, and which gave the poetry-reading public something new to think about.

At the outbreak of war in 1914 there had been a wild upsurging of patriotic emotion which Rupert Brooke expressed in his sonnet called *Peace*, which seemed to be the last word on the subject.

Now, God be thanked Who has matched us with His hour,
And caught our youth, and wakened us from sleeping,
With hand made sure, clear eye, and sharpened power,
To turn, as swimmers into cleanness leaping,
Glad from a world grown old and cold and weary,
Leave the sick hearts that honour could not move,
And half-men, and their dirty songs and dreary,
And all the little emptiness of love!

But Brooke did not live on to see the mass-slaughters of the Western Front, and the long slow stalemate which lasted until 1918. The poets who had been posted to the French front had a horrible awakening from this patriotic vision. They began to tell the truth about the war in no uncertain terms; far from being an honourable and glorious enterprise, they found it a stupid and meaningless butchery carried on by the politicians and the militarists to advance their own ends. Brooke and the others had sung the glories of war. The poetry-publics were staggered when Sassoon and Graves, Read and Owen, Robert

Nichols and Osbert Sitwell began to send them their cruel impressionistic pictures of the truth behind these poetic abstractions. Herbert Read's portrait of the 'Happy Warrior' seemed almost a piece of indecent exposure:

> His wild heart beats with painful sobs,
> His strained hands clench an ice-cold rifle,
> His aching jaws grip a hot parched tongue,
> And his wide eyes search unconsciously
>
> He cannot shriek
>
> Bloody saliva
> Dribbles down his shapeless jacket.
>
> I saw him stab
> And stab again
> A well-killed Boche.
>
> This is the happy warrior,
> This is he. . . .

It was not a portrait that the public at home wanted to see; they were happier with the newspaper fictions. But the poets flung it in their faces. Osbert Sitwell's pictures of men 'blown to patches of bleeding flesh' hanging on the barbed wire between the lines, were too faithful a record of reality for people not to accept them. People began to feel guilty about the causes of the war. A feeling of guilt about the collective irresponsibility which had caused the war was beginning to be felt on all sides.

> If I were fierce, and bald, and short of breath,
> I'd live with scarlet Majors at the Base,
> And speed glum heroes up the line to death.
> You'd see me with my puffy petulant face,
> Guzzling and gulping in the best hotel,
> Reading the Roll of Honour. 'Poor young chap',

I'd say—'I used to know his father well;
Yes, we've lost heavily in this last scrap.'
And when the war is done and youth stone dead,
I'd toddle safely home and die—in bed.

(*Base Details:* SASSOON)

Poetry as directly aimed as this could not be missed. The second group of war poets were also, for the great part, Georgians; at any rate some of them had been represented in the Georgian anthologies. But the war as subject matter was too important to waste: people must be made to realize what it meant.

You love us when we're heroes, home on leave,
Or wounded in a mentionable place.
You worship decorations; you believe
That chivalry redeems the war's disgrace.
You make us shells. You listen with delight,
By tales of dirt and danger fondly thrilled.
You crown our distant ardours while we fight,
And mourn our laurelled memories when we're killed.
You can't believe that British troops 'retire'
When hell's last horror breaks them, and they run,
Trampling the terrible corpses—blind with blood.
    O German mother dreaming by the fire,
    While you are knitting socks to send your son
    His face is trodden deeper in the mud.

(*The Glory of Women:* SASSOON)

The disgust and disillusion of these war-poets was afterwards carried forward under another head—that of prose. Aldington, Sassoon, Graves, Blunden all wrote prose-books about the experience of war: but their poetry was far more moving in its bitterness, in the sharpness of its style, and in the directness of its attack. But the war robbed us of at least two poets of the first rank, Wilfred Owen and Edward Thomas. Owen's indictment of war was no less forthright than that of the others, but his poetry was full-

133

grown at this time, and he achieved a certain maturity of compassion, a certain resignation which made it more complete. He was too humble to accuse anyone of guilt; he felt too strongly his own share in the general guilt of the community. And while his work carried the full force of the poetic indictment of war, it was never shrill. Its gravity and controlled emotion mark it off from the rest. Perhaps this makes it even more bitter.

### FRAGMENT: THE ABYSS OF WAR

As bronze may be much beautified
By lying in the damp dark soil,
So men who fade in dust of warfare fade
Fairer, and sorrow blooms their soul.

Like pearls which noble women wear
And, tarnishing, awhile confide
Unto the old salt sea to feed,
Many return more lustrous than they were.

But his actual descriptions of life in the fighting-line were no less violent and brilliantly coloured than the work of the other poets. His description of a gas casualty, for example, in *Dulce et decorum est.* . . .

If in some smothering dreams, you too could pace
Behind the wagon that we flung him in,
And watch the white eyes writhing in his face,
His hanging face, like a devil's sick of sin,
If you could hear, at every jolt, the blood
Come gargling from his froth-corrupted lungs
Bitten as the cud
Of vile, incurable sores on innocent tongues,—
My friend, you would not tell with such high zest
To children ardent for some desperate glory,
The old lie: *Dulce et decorum est*
*Pro patria mori.*

It is a very different version of Kipling's *If* to the one which was expected from the poets who saw themselves as 'swimmers into cleanness leaping'.

Edward Thomas who was, like Owen, killed in the war, was perhaps the greatest of the Georgian poets; the distinguishing label of 'Georgian', indicates simply the kind of subject-matter with which he was most at home—country-side matters. He wrote little about the war, and indeed the greater part of his verse passed unnoticed until his poetry was collected and issued in a single volume in 1922. In the same year appeared Wilfred Owen's *Collected Poems*, and the influence of both poets was not felt until then.

Thomas is a quietist and nature-lover whose clean and delicate workmanship deserves study even in those poems where he is not at his best. He reminds one of George Herbert in the still piety of his workmanship—yet his themes are never made sentimental by reference to emotional abstractions like God or Mother Nature. He is a poet who develops the concrete to its highest power by delicacy of observation—and allows the reader to feel the 'otherness' of atmosphere without intruding a specific explanatory text or a set of religious beliefs. He is a pure contemplative.

RAIN

Rain, midnight rain, nothing but the wild rain
On this bleak hut, and solitude, and me
Remembering again that I shall die
And neither hear the rain nor give it thanks
For washing me cleaner than I have been
Since I was born into this solitude.
Blessed are the dead that the rain rains upon:
But here I pray that none whom once I loved
Is dying tonight, or lying still awake
Solitary, listening to the rain,
Either in pain or thus in sympathy

Helpless among the living and the dead,
Like a cold water among broken reeds,
Myriads of broken reeds all still and stiff,
Like me who have no love which this wild rain
Has not dissolved except the love of death,
If love it be for what is perfect and
Cannot, the tempest tells me, disappoint.

Behind the artlessness of Thomas' statement and the simplicity of his technique lies an extraordinary and felicitous gift of ear and feeling for emotional line. His poems balance up beautifully. Their colouring is restrained and yet just sharp enough to carry the emotion he wants to convey.

Writing of poetry and the poet in 1917, T. S. Eliot says: 'What happens is a continual surrender of himself as he is at the moment to something which is more valuable. The progress of an artist is a continual self sacrifice, a continual extinction of personality'. It is this self-surrender that gives the final authority, the deathless bloom to good poetry; in the light of what we know about the changing conception of the ego under the influence of Freud, Jung and Groddeck we may well ask ourselves whether this idea is not the mainspring behind much of the poetry of today. You may say that all great poets have understood this matter and followed out this curve of depersonalization in their work; but never have they been so critically and intellectually conscious of the process as they are today; and never have they been faced with a dispersed ego provided by science and philosophy. Never has their message been more accessible to ordinary people or more urgently connected with the state of the world as it must be if it is not to perish.

The work of the Sitwells which began to appear at about this time fits very naturally into the period beside the poetry of Peter Quennell who, though his early promise delighted, has published nothing since this time.

Of these three notable writers, a sister and two brothers, Osbert became and has remained more famous for prose than for poetry, while Sacheverell and Edith were primarily poets—though both wrote poetic prose of force and beauty. Today Edith Sitwell is by far the greatest poet of the family, though she herself seems inclined to value the work of her brother more highly than her own.

Deeply influenced by the Symbolists, Edith Sitwell was also very conscious of the eighteenth-century aristocratic tradition. She tried to marry up these influences and to bring her poetry up to date by adding some of the harshness and bitterness of the twentieth-century attitude. The weakness of her early verse lay perhaps in the limited range of its subject-matter, which too often left her at the mercy of her technical virtuosity—a virtuosity and brilliance of treatment which was uniquely her own.

> Perhaps if I too lie down in the mud
> Beneath tumbrils rolling
> And mad skulls galloping
> Far from their bunches of nerves that dance
> And caper among these slums and prance—
> Beneath the noise of that hell that rolls
> I shall forget the shrunken souls
> The eyeless mud squealing 'God is dead,'
> Starved men (bags of wind), and the harlot's tread,
> The heaven turned into monkey-hide
> By Lady Bamburgher's dancing fleas,
> Her rotting-parties and death-slack ease. . . .

Her verse of this period is full of the romantic vocabulary of another century: 'tumbrils', 'fauns', 'satyrs', 'dolphins'. Much of it is weak, and much mannered. But what is really new about it is its sense of pattern, and its strange new tone-effects, which are mostly achieved by the marriage of unlikely nouns and adjectives. 'Blunt rain' falls in these poems, and breezes are 'pig-snouted'. Much of her subject-matter was concerned with the impressions of childhood—at that time almost the private preserve of Walter de La Mare; but in her work childhood is quite a different affair—it is seen through the eyes of a Dadaist. Her nursery-rhymes are shrill and fantastic where de La Mare's are wistful and evocative:

> Rose Castles
> Those bustles
> Beneath parasols seen!
> Flat blondine pearls
> Rondine curls
> Seem. Bannerols sheen
> The brave tartan
> Waves' Spartan
> Domes—(Crystal Palaces)
> Where like fallacies
> Die the calices
> Of the water-flowers green.
> Said the Dean
> To the Queen
> On the tartan wave seen:
> 'Each chilly
> White lily
> Has her own crinoline,
> And the seraphs recline
> On divans divine
> In a smooth seventh heaven of
>     polished pitch-pine.'

Edith Sitwell's later development has placed her, in authority and distinction, beside Yeats, but even these early verses exerted a great influence over young writers. I say 'young' advisedly because it must not be imagined that these new voices were generally recognized as belonging to great poets until the thirties. The greater part of the poetry-reading public looked upon these experiments with distaste, and showed a distinct preference for the main line of Georgian tradition—as any anthology of that period will show. Postwar disgust and disillusion did not flower until the war-novelists and the satirists began to make headway about 1925; yet even then many readers and writers were only too happy to sink back into the comfortable pantheistic quietism of the nature poets. Blunden, Drinkwater and Shanks seemed far saner and far more reliable poets than these dissidents. The Sitwells and Eliot were considered dangerous innovators. If you should consult an average anthology of the time—let us say *Poems of Today*: First Series, published by Sidgwick and Jackson (thirty-first impression: 1925)—you find fairly representative poetry by Yeats, Bridges, Masefield, Belloc, Chesterton, Davies, Drinkwater, Brooke, Blunden. You do not find the Sitwells or Ezra Pound or Eliot represented here. In their place you find about fifteen authors of trite little poems who have not been heard of since.

In 1929 appeared Harold Monro's own anthology *Twentieth Century Poetry*—which must certainly be considered the best guide to the poetry of the time. There is hardly a poet or a tendency that does not find a place in the pages of this model anthology. In his preface Monro writes:

> Today we each have our *Waste Land*, and the strong influence of Mr. T. S. Eliot, and a few other poets, chiefly unacknowledged in Georgian circles, is more indicative of future tendencies than any other recognizable Signpost. I should say that just as A. E. Housman was a very powerful influence up to 1920, so T. S. Eliot will be up to 1940.

The new poets, then, were making inroads upon the established tradition; but this is not to say that their elders were not also producing good work. Nor does it suggest that the younger traditionals were not holding their own successfully. Within the covers of Monro's anthology you will find the lyrics of James Joyce, the rough-surfaced free verse of D. H. Lawrence and the harpoon-like verses of Roy Campbell—to mention three writers of very different calibre; you will find the meteoric flashes of Gerard Manley Hopkins side by side with the country drowsings of Blunden and Drinkwater; lastly you will find the shrill and jagged verses of Edith Sitwell beside the ironic and startling comments of T. S. Eliot upon the world. But the full force of innovation was not properly felt and experienced until the emergence during the thirties of another group of poets—the 'New Signatures' group.

Meanwhile the older poets like John Masefield and Robert Bridges continued to write, though they did not experiment. Masefield's narrative verse had made him already famous before the war; Robert Bridges was to score a great success with his *The Testament of Beauty* published in 1929. Throughout his long working life (his first book was published in 1873) Bridges had developed and consolidated his position, though he had added little lyric poetry to his early work. His last long poem is an attempt to sum up his views upon the nature of imagination and its relation to poetry. It is not by any means a great poem though its technical idiosyncrasies make it well worth studying as an example of how far experiment had begun to affect even the most traditional of poets at this time. Its subject-matter too (it is an inquiry into the nature of Beauty) shows that the author was acquainted with most of the developments in twentieth-century metaphysics—that he was abreast of the tide in his reading. For a poet so old and so firmly fixed in his tradition the experimental treatment of the subject in *The Testament of Beauty* was truly revolutionary; but the verse does not wear well, and today most of the technical tricks Bridges used seem wilful and artificial. Yet the poem enjoyed a very great public success, as Masefield's *The Everlasting Mercy* had in 1911.

So if we, changing Plato's old difficult term, should re-name his Ideas Influences, there is none would miss his meaning nor, by nebulous logic, wish to refute his doctrine that indeed there are eternal Essences that exist in themselves, supreme efficient causes of the thoughts of men.

> *What is Beauty? saith my sufferings then.*—I answer
> the lover and poet in my loose alexandrines:
> Beauty is the highest of all these occult influences,
> The quality of appearances that thru' the sense
> wakeneth spiritual emotion in the mind of man....

It is not very successful, either as a statement of a metaphysic or as poetry. Bridges turned aside from the exhaustion of shrillness of the century and tried to build a cobweb of verse about the idea of Beauty. He tried to trace its function and relationship to man, and to indicate that behind the idea of Beauty lay another idea: that of the personality's integration with the universe surrounding it.

For all the novelties in spelling and the 'loose alexandrines' the poem is more remarkable for subject-matter than for the quality of the workmanship. And yet it has certain positive qualities which forbid us to pass it over entirely; there is some of the graceful and lucid Bridges of the late nineties in it. It might have been better done in prose: it is certainly too didactic: its mannerisms are irritating. Yet when every qualification has been made there is something left. *The Testament of Beauty* is one of those poems which will have to be rediscovered and reinterpreted by a generation which is no longer irritated by the manner in which it is written. It is more ambitious than the other successful poems of its epoch (like the poems of Humbert Wolfe or V. Sackville-West's long poem *The Land* which enjoyed wide popularity in 1926).

But with the publication of T. S. Eliot's *The Waste Land* in 1922 a corner had been turned, although only the young writers seemed to have realized the fact. The general public was more conservative, and refused to countenance anything which was not the orthodox nature-poetry of the day.

## CHAPTER 7

# T. S. ELIOT

THE film is the great neglected art-form of today. It has not realized its function, which is to marry images seen and images heard, marry poetry and picture, into a new artistic form: it is still nailed to the cross of naturalism, while its content is, in a crude sort of way, the content of those old moralities which occupied the position later taken by the dramas of Kyd and Marlowe. Yet despite these defects the cinema is an admirable metaphor for us to choose when we come to discuss modern poetry. There are many analogies of technique between even the worst film and the best modern poem: and the comparison is invaluable if we are to get any sense out of *The Waste Land*, the poem by T. S. Eliot which has exercised such a great influence over modern writing in England.

If the puzzled average reader could surrender himself to it as he surrenders himself to a film he might feel the visual transitions of the images and the plot for what they are—skilful organizations of the author's moods. Perhaps you remember the long track-shot in *Gone With the Wind* where the camera shuttles slowly across the battlefield, picking up here and there different items in the catalogue of war—a charred bivouac, a huddle of corpses, an over-turned cart. Your eye takes in these images and interprets through them the meaning of war, of disaster, of blood-shed, without the intellectual content of the picture being explicit. Then again, in another film, *Citizen Kane*, you perhaps remember the closing sequence where the camera explores the crowded cellars of the millionaire tycoon's palace: it roves slowly over the immense rubbish-heap of meaningless statuary, chairs, lamp-standards, crockery, furniture, books, beds, china, looking for the one small integrating symbol which will explain the tragedy of the millionaire's life—the sledge which he used as a boy and which has been lying down here forgotten. Here again your eye takes in this immense collection of rubbish and your mind interprets it for you in terms of the drama you have seen. A life devoted to possessions has no meaning, you find yourself thinking. How much junk is there in *my* lumber-room? Didn't this wretched man realize that happiness was not in having but in being? These are the sort of intellectual rationalizations which your brain weaves as it interprets the picture. But whereas in the film one is given a naturalistic pattern to which the image is subsidiary, in a poem like *The Waste Land* the task of interpretation becomes more difficult; one is called upon to reconstruct *Citizen Kane*, so to speak, from this single track-shot of the junk he has collected in his cellar.

Yet from the point of view of technique the poem is exactly the same sort of thing—the camera pans slowly over the whole intellectual and spiritual battlefield of the twentieth century, picking up here a prayer wheel, there a quotation from Tacitus or Baudelaire, stopping to peep into a medieval missal or to eavesdrop upon the love affair of a city typist, to wander down a grimy London street, or to remind itself that the Elizabethans, gorgeously clad, walked this exhausted stage on which the modern man (in search of belief) wanders. *The Waste Land* embalms the life of the twentieth century in a series of images, some disgusting, some beautiful, some vague, some sharp as crystal.

The trouble with the common reader is that he knows that the twentieth century is a battlefield, but he does not know what the battle is about: he is unaware of the real issues involved in the struggles which the poem mirrors. The allusions to books he has not read, to authors he has only heard of, irritate him and make him feel that perhaps he is the victim of an intellectual leg-pull. This impression is confirmed when he realizes that the prevailing tone of the poem is irony. Poetry, for the average man, is still situated halfway between uplift and pure sensation. He hunts for a plot, for a structure, and finds instead flight after flight of carefully woven images, sequences of moods which at first look haphazard, but later come to be recognized as a skilful patterning of feelings.

This is the point at which the critic steps in and begins his learned dissertation upon Eliot's early influences— Baudelaire, Donne, Laforgue. Usually they explain little. The great poet always borrows, but he always pays back with interest; and his production is something more than the sum of his borrowings. Certainly of the three poets mentioned above only Laforgue might have recognized *The Waste Land* as a stepchild. But he might have criticized it on the grounds that the material was intellectually controlled and shaped towards a predetermined end. It was not free fantasy in the fullest sense. It betrayed intellectual organization—a factor which stamps it as a product of the twentieth century. It is one thing to use free-association and images before Freud and Frazer: it is quite another thing to use them when they have become conscious, when their value is clear even if their meaning is not. The poet of the post-Freudian era finds it impossible to surrender to his unconscious in the way that Rimbaud did. His world is moving in another direction. He is learning to interpret his material and bend it to a new use in his life. This growing awareness is what separates the poet of this century from the poet of the last—and here I should add that in 1922 (the year of *Ulysses'* publication) we also have Lawrence's *Fantasia of the Unconscious*. It was round about this time that the full impact of Freud and Frazer was beginning to be felt. It was natural enough that the reaction should be against the former rather than for him;

Freud's mechanistic method of dealing with his findings had yet to be modified and reinterpreted by the other great psycho-analysts Jung, Otto Rank and others. But the main lines of thought on the question of the unconscious, the main structure of Frazer's thesis, were very much under discussion at this time. I am reminded here of three other names, Aldous Huxley, Robert Graves and D. H. Lawrence: all betrayed a knowledge of psychoanalysis in their writings of this period.

Now Eliot appears to owe no debt to Freud, yet it is worth noting that in *The Waste Land* the personae behave like characters in a dream, changing their attributes and shapes; and that Tiresias is a bisexual symbol. In his note Eliot says:

> Tiresias, although a mere spectator and not indeed a 'character', is yet the most important personage in the poem, uniting all the rest. Just as the one-eyed merchant, seller of currants, melts into the Phoenician sailor, and the latter is not wholly distinct from Ferdinand Prince of Naples, so all the women are one woman, and the two sexes meet in Tiresias. What Tiresias *sees*, in fact, is the substance of the poem.

Tiresias is camera-man, then. But he is not fixed chronologically—he can move about in history and in time; he can become a modern city-man, a medieval, or an ancient Greek at will. *The Waste Land* is his spiritual autobiography, his search through the junk-heap of modern culture for an integrating principle. Why has it been lost? Where does the clue lie? And in setting himself to pose, and if possible, to answer this question Eliot calls up all his massive erudition, his prodigious reading, to serve as an illustration to the text. This is what gives the poem its baffling and anomalous appearance. The search goes on on several diverging planes: autobiography, archæology, mythology, religion. And the camera moves backwards and forwards with a relentless shuttling movement over legend, belief and symbol. No sooner does it pick up a figure than it dissolves into its attributes, as a Greek God does when you try and find his essential meaning by consulting a dictionary of mythology. Eliot's characters, like many Greek Gods, enjoy multiple attributes, often opposing ones.

> His intellect, (says a critic), was trained at Harvard, Paris and Oxford almost entirely in the pre-war period (1906-15) when the spirit of tradition was stronger than now and Universities more content to be trustees of knowledge. Moreover, he was chiefly concerned with literature and philosophy—that is, in pre-scientific learning, which we value because it belongs to every age, and relies on intuition, or on insight into the unchanging values of human nature. He was also much influenced, then or later, by the prophetic books of the Bible, and the esoteric teaching of Zoroaster, Buddha and Lao-Tzu. He was something of a mystic; by temperament and training dissatisfied at the 'ignorant knowledge' much favoured of his own generation. It is not surprising that he was also a student, almost a disciple, of I. Babbitt and G. Santayana.

*The Waste Land* is a jeremiad against a civilization that values knowledge above wisdom, words above The Word. If the keynote is disillusion and negation, as critics have said, it is because we recognize that the cap fits. The modern city-man, heir to all the ages, possessor of as great a science and of an accumulated knowledge greater than anything the world has seen, is in an *impasse*. How can he organize all this material in such a way as to give his life meaning? The problem was urgent in 1922. It became still more urgent in the decade that followed. Today it is the only really serious problem facing us.

The clue to this difficult poem, then, lies in understanding its objectives, not in losing ourselves among the notes in the appendix. It is idle to track down the references unless you feel the general drift of the argument—

for the cross-referencing is really one of moods—and unless you submit yourself to the moods you will find the references more trouble than help. We speak of 'understanding' poems as if they were built up in sections like a child's Meccano bridge; but the truth is that we can never fully understand a good poem until we can fully understand ourselves. Our job then is to make ourselves accessible to the poem and use both sensibility and intelligence to this end. This implies a condition of passive alertness. It does not imply frantic activity with note-book and pencil. That comes later.

Now if *The Waste Land* were scripted as a radio-play is we might find passages more easy to feel. I don't know how far I shall be running foul of contemporary criticism by suggesting that most of Eliot's poetry is essentially dramatic, and that his development as a playwright is apparent even in *The Waste Land*. But that is how it seems to me. He uses narrative and description to offset the main theme which is autobiographical. Inner and outer interchange the whole time. Suppose we arranged the poem for a number of voices—would that not give one some insight into the sort of poem it is? Since we are busy with trying to understand it we should not be afraid of taking liberties. We have only the professional critics to fear.

(*A Woman's Voice against fading music*)
April is the cruellest month, breeding
Lilacs out of the dead land, mixing
Memory and desire, stirring
Dull roots with spring rain.
Winter kept us warm, covering
Earth in forgetful snow, feeding
A little life with dried tubers.

(*A younger Voice, eagerly*)
Summer surprised us, coming over the Starnbergersee
With a shower of rain; we stopped in the colonnade,

(*She sighs*)

    And went on in sunlight, into the Hofgarten,
    And drank coffee, and talked for an hour.

(*Fade into soft buzz of conversation against which a hoarse, plump voice, that of a rich middle-aged Jewess, shall we say? announces volubly*)

    Bin gar keine Russin, stamm' aus Litauen, echt deutsch.

(*The second voice goes on breathlessly as a distant band begins to play an old waltz*)

    And when we were children, staying at the archduke's,
    My cousin's, he took me out on a sled,
    And I was frightened. He said, Marie

(*The music becomes louder. She raises her voice*)

    Marie, hold on tight. And down we went.

(*The music gives a bang and the hoarse plump voice says with false conversational animation*)

    In the mountains (*she sighs*) there you feel free.
    I read, much of the night, and go south in the winter.

(*The noise of trains shunting and the howl of their whistles from some distant goodsyard. Against the soft puff-puff of escaping steam and the rattle of wheels rises the grave voice of the Commentator, a man*)

    What are the roots that clutch, what branches grow
    Out of this stony rubbish? Son of man,
    You cannot say, or guess, for you know only
    A heap of broken images, where the sun beats,
    And the dead tree gives no shelter. . . .

I am, of course, taking great liberties with my subject, but they are justified if such a method helps you to actualize the poem and give value to its images. Heard in terms of radio you would be unable to stop every few lines to ask yourself what this word means, or that. You would be forced to accept the poem as a significant whole. It is

the naturalistic setting which the common reader misses in
*The Waste Land* and which, for some reason or other, he is
loth to let his imagination supply. Both film and radio,
however, give us a clue to the technique, and we would be
foolish not to make use of it.

(*A Girl's Voice*)
   You gave me hyacinths first a year ago;
   They called me the hyacinth girl.

(*A Man's Voice*)
   —Yet, when we came back, late, from the Hyacinth garden,
   Your arms full, and your hair wet, I could not

(*He breaks off and continues in a whisper*)
   Speak, and my eyes failed, I was neither
   Living nor dead, and I knew nothing,
   Looking into the heart of light, the silence.

(*A mocking woman's voice*)
   Oed' und leer das Meer

(*She utters the words very slowly, like a spell, drawing out the long 'e'
in 'leer' and 'Meer'.*)

(*The noise of curtain-rings, as if a curtain were being drawn aside
upon some dark recess. A cultivated, fruity voice—the voice one hears
on the news-films—says*)
   Madame Sosostris, famous clairvoyante,
   Had a bad cold, nevertheless
   Is known to be the wisest woman in Europe,
   With a wicked pack of cards. Here, said she,

(*The voice of the old fortune-teller, very slowly, in deep muffled tones*)
   Is your card, the drowned Phoenician Sailor,
   (Those are pearls that were his eyes. Look!)
   Here is Belladonna, the Lady of the Rocks,
   The lady of situations. . . .

*The Waste Land* was indeed written for a number of voices—but they are the voices of the unconscious, and if we are to get the hang of it we must supply them for ourselves when we read it. We are only given the raw materials. The poem turns the whole time like a mirror, taking us backwards and forwards between reminiscence and description, between the present and the past: and packed closely into it, among the images, are the fragments of the culture to which we belong, our art, our religion, our mythology.

Why has the central significance of these been lost?—or at least why do we feel that they have been lost? In my earlier lectures I tried to provide you with some clues. Psychology has dispersed the old fixed ego, has disintegrated it and joined it up with myths. Science and metaphysics have provided a new attitude to Time and continuity. Belonging to a city-culture which we have made, we still long for something else. We know that the city-man is doomed.

> What is the city over the mountains
> Cracks and reforms and bursts in the violet air
> Falling towers
> Jerusalem Athens Alexandria
> Vienna London
> Unreal

And here if you care to add the mad laughter of women in insane asylums, it would give you a fitting background to:

> A woman drew her long black hair out tight
> And fiddled whisper music on those strings
> And bats with baby faces in the violet light
> Whistled, and beat their wings
> And crawled head downward down a blackened wall
> And upside down in air were towers
> Tolling reminiscent bells, that kept the hours
> And voices singing out of empty cisterns and
>     exhausted wells.

Eliot has not acknowledged any debt to Freud; yet, if we must believe the notes to this poem he owes much to anthropology. 'Not only the title,' he says, 'but much of the symbolism of the poem were suggested by Miss Jessie L. Weston's book on the Grail Legend: *From Ritual to Romance . . .* To another work of anthropology I am indebted in general, one which has influenced our generation profoundly; I mean *The Golden Bough*'. First published in 1890, this huge study of animism was finished in its present form between 1911-15. It not only provided a link between contemporary and primitive religious beliefs —it provided the psychologists with a sort of stock-pot of primitive thought, much of which they were finding still active in the unconscious of modern city-man. It provided Eliot with a frame of symbolic reference. But the old Tiresias, the bisexual symbol situated at the heart of the poem, suggests something else.

We know that the investigations into the unconscious lead us to attribute bisexuality to the psyche; it also reminds us that the Eastern Gods were bisexual. Scientific fact and myth marry up at this point. But there is another religious or mystical idea underlying this idea of bisexuality. I am thinking of the Buddhist quotations that bring *The Waste Land* to a close, and suggest a possible solution to the dilemma in which Western Man finds himself. We have seen that Eliot was influenced by Eastern teaching before he became an Anglo-Catholic. Perhaps the latter event came hard upon the discovery that in all religions the mystical objective is the same one—the gnosis or understanding of the mystery of man's essential being.

Among some of the older gnostic fragments, the Logoi which the compilers of our sacred books rejected, we find reflections of this same idea, which must be as old as Lao Tzu, which must have been known to Plato and Pythagoras. We read, for example, the following: 'When the Lord was asked by a certain man, When should His kingdom come, He saith unto him: When two shall be one, and the without and the within, and the male with the female, neither male or female.' I would like to think that in Tiresias we had a symbol of this kind, pointing towards the future integration which lies beyond the hills of science and metaphysics, anthropology, and even perhaps art itself. From this point of view, then, the poem is something more than an expression of 'utter negation and disgust'. It does suggest a possible integration of the spirit of man— but meanwhile it invites you to look at our city-culture for what it is, without idealism or sentimentality. Sex: the seduction of a city typist by her pimply boy-friend; history, myth, art. . . . It is a world without roots, without values, becoming fuller every day with the voices of crooners and dictators.

Meanwhile these strange modern characters flit backwards and forwards across the scene, each accompanied by his mythical archetype; the astrologer, the palmist, the city typist, the Smyrna merchant. How can the artist get them back into their mythological frame so that they become parts of a significant picture? This is the problem, not only of *The Waste Land*, but of the culture of which it is an expression. The values of two thousand years of civilization all seem to have become shipwrecked upon the shores of the twentieth century. Snatches of jazz and the wild laughter from bars punctuate the poem, like the sad distant wailing of saxaphones that you hear late at night from some underground cellar, or the wailing of love-sick cats. Voices intervene, one telescoped into another, uttering snatches of half-overheard conversation—like those voices talking in the other room which you hear while you are lying sick in bed. What do they say? What do they mean? If the values are all telescoped it is to show exactly how meaningless our age finds them: everything is accessible, from the esoteric teachings of the saints, the doctrines of the Chinese, to the treasures of Greek or Renaissance art. Yet, having all this at our doorsteps, we are still conscious of a great chasm yawning between values and action.

*The Waste Land* is not an attempt to retreat into history or myth, but a bold attempt to face the implications behind it, and to see whether or not there is some way of accommodating it and enriching ourselves with it. So although the keynote of the poem seems to be exhaustion and negation it leaves us with a hope. . . .

> To Carthage then I came
> Burning burning burning burning
> O Lord Thou pluckest me out
> O Lord Thou pluckest
>
> burning

The juxtaposition of St. Augustine and Buddha is not, if we are to believe the notes, an accident; the values implied in the teaching of both lie underneath the questions which we are asking ourselves today. And under the main theme of despair we hear this message repeated over and over again. *The Waste Land* draws a faithful picture of the human condition, but it also suggests that there are ways out of our present dilemma.

*Ash Wednesday* was published in 1930, and struck a note of religious affirmation suitable enough to a poet who had declared himself a royalist in politics, a classicist in art, and an Anglo-Catholic in religion. For the next ten years Eliot devoted himself to criticism and to the resurrection of the verse-play—a task which he performed single-handed with *The Rock* (1934), *Murder in the Cathedral* (1935) and *The Family Reunion* (1939), and in which several younger poets followed his lead.

In 1936 he published the first of the four long poems he calls *Quartets*, and which contain perhaps his ripest and most profound work. Here the poetic struggle which one sees in *The Waste Land* is resolved both on the plane of technique and on the plane of the spirit. The poet and the man have come to terms, have accepted a creative compromise which enriches both the work and the values it depends upon. The exhaustion and the despair have both gone, and these four cathedral pieces, with their intense devotional flavour and measured pace, indicate a new orientation, a new use and integration of present and past. The *Four Quartets* rank beside the best religious poetry in the language, beside the best of the later Donne and Herbert.

Once again the various themes are skilfully woven and matched, but this time it is not a portrait of the age which the poet is attempting; he is recapturing his own past and describing it in the light of the new timeless time, past, present and future, which science and religion alike have brought within the reach of the ordinary person. The Catholic critics have been extremely busy explaining the symbolism of the poems and the intentions of the author according to the faith they hold. We cannot say they are wrong to do so. But it would be equally true to say that the poems are something more than sectarian propaganda— the current carries us back into an era long before the Western Churches were founded, into an era of speculation about life, and the meaning of time.

Eliot's mind is one which inhabits the sixth century B.C. as easily as it accommodates itself to the Middle Ages—or to tomorrow. The point is worth making since these fine poems are likely to suffer at the hands of two sorts of critics: those who are eager to read into them a purely sectarian meaning, and those who suffer from an anti-clerical bias. Both must in the nature of things be unjust to the poetry as poetry, and to the belief as belief.

> Time present and time past
> Are both perhaps present in time future,
> And time future contained in time past.

If all time is eternally present
All time is unredeemable.
What might have been is an abstraction
Remaining a perpetual possibility
Only in a world of speculation.
What might have been and what has been
Point to one end, which is always present. . . .

These opening lines from *Burnt Norton* will remind you of much that I have already said about time: time as the physicist is beginning to understand it, time as Bruno thought of it. All time suspended in an instant of time, always renewing itself yet standing quite still. This is the main preoccupation of the four poems. But in the light of this new awareness, this new time, everything changes its shape and meaning—the past no less than the future, and the poet begins the long trek back through memory and association, to try and paint a picture of his life in terms of the new time he has experienced. It is a time which contains all opposites. . . .

Neither from nor towards; at the still point, there
                                      the dance is,
But neither arrest nor movement. And do not
                                      call it fixity.
Where past and future are gathered. . . .

You will remember perhaps that I mentioned opposites being equal in the unconscious, and that for the physicist also it was necessary to marry opposites in order to arrive at a picture of reality. This is something as old as religion or mysticism—and the curious thing about the world today is that these extraordinary descriptions of a territory which we thought inhabited only by visionaries and mystics, are now coming upon us with something like scientific approval. This is what I meant when I spoke about the sciences and religions converging upon a single objective. One group speaks of equations and pragmatic truths, the other speaks of revelation: but they are reaching a point now when they are forced to admit the validity of each other's claims. Meanwhile, however, the individual's problem has remained the same. How to grow up and accept this new reality, and turn it to good account in the individual life of man? It has always been accessible (at many points you will see that the *Four Quartets* re-state the formulæ of Lao Tzu and other mystics of the past). But this is a problem for which there lies only an individual solution. It is each man for himself. Eliot's solution may not be valid for anyone but himself. I am trying to suggest that we should avoid searching these poems for dogma, and accept them as descriptions of fact.

Technically these poems owe a great deal to the experiments Eliot has made in verse-drama (and about which I would like to speak at some other time). He uses a long, unstressed line which looks at first formless, until you realize that he has married it to the inflexions of a conversational tone. The gearing is not very high—and the full weight of the poetry lies behind the multiple impact of simple statement, almost conversationally introduced. The writing conforms to all we have said about the cyclic art of this time, only it depends not on the packing of sounds together so much as the packing of ideas. This is, at bottom, a dialectical problem—how to convey a state for which words are inadequate? How to name a reality which is no longer itself once you qualify it with a name? How to state something which is beyond opposites in a language which is based upon opposites?

Eliot, in order to be true to this reality as he describes it, must adopt a negative-positive attitude. Since statement qualifies, he must at once correct it by introducing its opposite and measuring its claims against what he has already said. So that the poem only *indicates* the object it is

regarding. It cannot circumscribe it within the inade-
quacies of linguistic equipment.

Meanwhile the poet summons up memory of his own
history, of the history of his family, and of the localities in
England which throw out connecting fibres to join up with
his own faith, and to remind him that faith and life alike
have inter-communicating roots. The resulting pattern
described by these four poems, with their changes of
measure, their elliptical turning and twisting, is one of
different types of time. Time as history, personal and
family history: time as suffering: time as the 'still centre',
the timeless moment when past present and future are
joined and compressed into one moment of vision. The
actual references, Little Gidding, Burnt Norton, and so on,
you already know. They are so to speak flags or markers,
which indicate each point of departure. They are both
incidental to the poem and at the same time useful point-
references to it. They describe, if you like, the key in
which the poem is written—they are key-signatures. Meanwhile, however,

> The detail of the pattern is movement,
> As in the figure of the ten stairs.
> Desire itself is movement
> Not in itself desirable;
> Love is itself unmoving,
> Only the cause and end of movement,
> Timeless and undesiring
> Except in the aspect of time
> Caught in the form of limitation
> Between un-being and being. . . .

The real triumph of the poems is in the technical feat
of recording ecstasy with intellectual control and detachment. The *Four Quartets* are not soft like Crashaw or jagged
like Donne. They are kept firmly within the intellectual
boundaries of the colouring and emotion the poet thought

most suited to the subject. In this sense they go a step beyond either Donne or Crashaw in their acceptance of the fact that opposites are identical. Under the terms of this metaphysic despair and ecstasy, love and hate—or any two opposites you care to name—are co-equals, sharers, partners. To let one have its head at the expense of the other would spoil the 'stillness' of the dance.

I am sorry if this sounds paradoxical. It is explicit not only in what the poet says with his long rows of antitheses, 'neither' against 'nor' and 'either' against 'or', but it is also clear in the struggle of his language to break free from the meshes of dialectic and soar. That it has form is due less to the purely technical considerations of its structure than to the quality of the state which is here expressed. It is a state which can only be expressed in negatives.

> In order to possess what you do not possess
> You must go by way of dispossession
> In order to arrive at where you are not
> You must go through the way in which you are not
> And what you do not know is the only thing you know
> And what you own is what you do not own
> And where you are is where you are not.

Critics have already pointed out the resemblance that this statement shares with certain writings of the mystics: indeed the passage above is said by the author to be a paraphrase of a fragment from St. John of the Cross. One critic, Hugh Gordon Porteous, compares some quotations from these poems with the writings of a Chinese mystic called Lao Tzu, and remarks on their resemblance. He adds:

> What could be more paradoxical than a poetic denial of poetry itself? Certainly it lends colour to a general notion that Mr. Eliot is emigrating from literature into the territory of the mystics. Elsewhere, to be sure, he confesses that

> to apprehend
> The point of intersection of the timeless
> With time, is an occupation for the saint.

And Mr. Auden, it will be recalled, once defined the saint as one

> to whom ethics have *almost* become aesthetics;

and the Poet's Prayer as

> Lord, teach me to write so well that I shall no longer want to.

The problem of the change in direction of modern poetry is one I have touched upon in my section called 'Beyond the Ego?' It deserves careful consideration in the light of the messages which we are receiving from the poets of today.

I said in an earlier lecture that if our ideas of Time were changed or disturbed it could not help but disturb our notions of life and death—since both concepts are tightly bound up with the idea of Time. So it is that in Eliot's *Four Quartets* we see the poet forced to evaluate his whole life and its meaning in terms of the new vision he has acquired—the new time which he is beginning to experience. From this still centre of contemplation, where all opposites are one, his lines of speculation widen out in rings, touching life, suffering, death, love—all those inadequate symbols by which we live and die without ever managing to completely define or circumscribe them. So that the central message of the poems lies in their re-evaluation of one individual life in terms of its historical and spiritual significance.

Of the impersonality and the peculiar qualities of T. S. Eliot's technique much has been written; while he himself has revealed much of his attitudes and ideas in his critical work. His technique has changed much since he wrote *The Waste Land*, yet he has lost none of his original power over words. The same cold monochrome technique is used with a much suppler line—the result of his practice with spoken verse. But the things he has to say are very much to the point, and phrases like 'What is living can only die' and 'Humility is endless' are not simply the calls of a muezzin to the faithful. They are the crystallizations of personal experience, statements of fact.

It may well be that what *The Waste Land* and *Gerontion* expressed for one generation *The Four Quartets* expresses for ours. Under its formal music the values seem clear: non-attachment instead of ironic detachment, non-action instead of inaction: and the marriage of opposites in the individual so that he can rise above the promptings of his dualistic ego. The idea of passivity, of letting-be, which we are rediscovering from the religious treatises of the East are still the source of much confusion.

'Mysticism' is still very much suspect by people who do not feel the desire to grow beyond the habitual and self-indulgent drowsings of their egos. Such people, and there are very many critics of literature among them, still maintain an obstinate idea that scientific reasoning is the answer to everything. Faced with a concept like Lao Tzu's 'non-action' they profess themselves puzzled. Yet as an idea it is no more complicated to grasp than the idea behind the scientific 'Principle of Least Action'. Indeed they are both the same thing, only what the mystic has posited for the personality of the individual the scientist has posited for the universe. I quote from Bertrand Russell's *ABC of Relativity*:

> All the laws of dynamics have been put together into one principle, called *The Principle of Least Action*. This states that, in passing from one state to another, a body chooses a route involving less action than any slightly different route—a law of cosmic laziness.

It would seem that there is rapidly being forged a common ground on which the scientist of today can meet the mystic; but for the latter the confessed object of his practice is the liberation of himself from the bondage of the ego.

> Liberation not less of love but expanding
> Of Love beyond desire, and so liberation
> From the future as well as the past.

But if the artist today is concerned with the transcending of his personality—if his confessed motives are a desire to reach desirelessness and a desire to grow beyond the ego—what is to happen to art? Is it to become pure metaphysics—or is it to die out gradually? At any rate some new transformation is foreshadowed in the new mystical departures. For until now art in the West was based upon the ego, upon the personality. Yet the ego has become diffused, broken down by philosophic and scientific enquiry; what reintegration is possible for the poet in order to recompose the ego, to give it value and shape? Eliot is not the only poet who recognizes this fact. In one of his earlier poems Stephen Spender writes:

> An 'I' can never be a great man.
> This known great one has weakness
> To friends is most remarkable for weakness
> His ill-temper at meals, his dislike of being contradicted,
> His only real pleasure fishing in ponds,
> His only real desire—forgetting.

> To advance from friends to the composite self
> Central 'I' is surrounded by 'I eating',
> 'I loving', 'I angry', 'I excreting',
> And the 'great I' planted in him
> Has nothing to do with all these,

The problem then of all modern poetry of any calibre and obscurity can best be seen in the light of our ideas about the ego and time. Out of our changing ideas about each will come the new poetry of tomorrow. Who can say what it will be like?

## CHAPTER 8

# GERARD MANLEY HOPKINS

THE first collection of poems by Hopkins was published in 1918 by Robert Bridges, who was the poet's literary executor, and who for many years before had been a rather dubious admirer of the fuliginous sensibility of this unknown Jesuit priest. The poems were received with great excitement, and Hopkins must be considered as having had a considerable effect upon the poets of the thirties; in many cases the effect was a bad one. A style so personal as that of Hopkins, a manner so closely married to the matter and content of what he wants to say simply cannot be imitated, though his terrific contrapuntal style lends itself easily enough as a model to a young poet without a formed style of his own.

Hopkins was a great discovery for the young, and the effect of his poems was felt quite as strongly as the effect of T. S. Eliot's *Waste Land*. His effect upon criticism was hardly less astonishing. 'It is evident,' wrote W. J. Turner, the poet and critic, 'that Hopkins resembled Keats more than any other English poet'. Another critic, however, has decided that he resembles Wordsworth much more closely. According to Walter de la Mare he reminds the reader of John Donne, while T. S. Eliot has done him the injustice of comparing him to Meredith. He has also been likened to Coventry Patmore, to Crashaw, and even to Walt Whitman. With so many comparisons already in the field one more cannot do any harm. There is much in Hopkins which reminds one of Emily Dickinson (1830-1886): the range of his subject-matter is nearly as small, while the formidable feeling of repression behind his cramped and compressed writing reminds one of the American poetess and her own crabbed and epigrammatic style. But while styles and sensibilities may be compared, poets must be granted the right to stand on their own as individuals. Hopkins himself, writing to Patmore, says:

> I scarcely understand you about reflected light: every true poet, I thought, must be original and originality a condition of poetic genius; so that each poet is like a species in nature (*not* an *individuum genericum* or *specificum*) and can never recur.

Hopkins was born in 1844 and died in 1889 of typhoid fever in Dublin. He provides an interesting and instructive example of how poets often defy the chronological critic by getting born at the wrong time. The effect of his work was not felt until Bridges' tardy publication in 1918—a publication whose preface indicated clearly enough the reservations that poets of Bridges' generation felt when they were confronted with experiment so daring and self-revelation so piercing.

Hopkins' poetry is the poetry of religious enthusiasm which combines the most daring verbal and intellectual skill with a strict discipline over form and emotion. There is nothing quite like it in the whole range of English poetry, though he obviously shares certain similarities of subject-matter with metaphysical and religious poets.

> God's most deep decree
> Bitter would have me taste: my taste was me;
> Bones built in me, flesh filled, blood brimmed the curse.
> Selfyeast of spirit a dull dough sours. I see
> The lost are like this, and their scourge to be
> As I am mine, their sweating selves; but worse.

The critic of Hopkins is faced with a difficult problem; he must first decide why he is a great poet, and then he must establish exactly why he is not among the greatest. Hopkins is not a 'universal' poet, in the sense that his verses while they exactly represent his spiritual sufferings and trials in verse of remarkable beauty, do not possess that gnomic flavour of a reality captured, tamed and experienced. 'I have been there,' writes T. S. Eliot, 'but I cannot say where.' Hopkins does not get 'there' though he suffers and strives to reach it: though all his poetry points like a dagger to the 'there' which he intuited as lying behind religious doubt and anxiety; but he never sends us a message from 'there'. He points, he exclaims, he suffers, he struggles: but he does not quite reach the territory in which and from which the 'universal' poet looks back, and occasionally drops us a message.

There is nothing genuinely other-worldly about Hopkins' poetry—except his preoccupation with the state of other-worldliness as subject-matter. He is the modern Tantalus, and his poetry is brimming with this unsatisfied thirst. No other poet has conveyed so brilliantly the feverish taste of spiritual hunger and thirst. A young Spanish critic suggests that Hopkins like Mallarmé is a poet of language and that his real importance is to language more than literature. There is something in this view.

Critics have occupied themselves with the unresolved struggle in Hopkins between what he felt to be his religious vocation and what he knew to be his poetic gift. How deep the struggle was we shall never know, but it is certain that a sensibility as acutely conscious of itself and the impact of the sensual world of feelings upon it, could not but feel cramped within the confines of an order of ideas which demanded intellectual and spiritual acquiescence, and left no room for the individual daring and bravery of the poetic temperament. We feel the deliberate cramping in his style with its terrific compression and its dislocations of syntax.

His poetry is like a great river forcing itself through a very narrow nozzle of a hose; his poetry comes out in jets and squirts. His rhyme schemes are rough-surfaced and held together by the tension of the 'sprung-rhythm' as he called it, which gives the impression sometimes of awkwardness, as if his Muse were walking about on stilts too tall for it. But whatever he did was grounded in form—a form so exact and so deliberate, that there is hardly a poem which does not seem to come off, to be a complete entity; while the extraordinary bravery of his surrender to direct impressions no less than that of his personal technique for capturing them, gives one a series of vivid shocks as one reads him. It is like watching a landscape lit by successive flashes of lightning. In his *Note-books* he writes:

> And when I ask where does all this throng and stack of being, so rich, so distinctive, so important, come from, nothing I see can answer me. And this whether I speak of human nature or of my individuality, my self-being. For human nature, being more highly pitched, selved and distinctive than anything in the world, can have been developed, evolved, condensed, from the vastness of the world not anyhow or by the working of common powers but only by one of finer or higher pitch and determination than itself and certainly than any that elsewhere we see, for this power had to force forward the starting or stubborn elements to the one pitch required. And this is much more true when we consider the mind; when I consider my self-being, my consciousness and feeling of myself, that taste of myself, of *I* and *me* above and in all things, which is more distinctive than the taste of ale or alum, more distinctive than the smell of walnutleaf or camphor, and is incommunicable by any means to another man (as when I was a child I used to ask myself: What must it be to be someone else?). Nothing else in nature comes near this unspeakable stress of pitch, distinctiveness, and selving, this selfbeing of my own.

It is a passage which might well have occurred among the writings of D. H. Lawrence, and it illustrates Hopkins'

central preoccupation, which was to master the terrific
sensation of being a separate person, cut off from the world
by an unbearable subjectivity of eye and mind. We do
not know if he would have agreed to such a statement himself. But the passage illustrates something more. It illustrates how even in prose Hopkins allowed the flood-waters
of his sensibility to run over and dislocate the formal
structure of statement.

The inversions, the double-words, the analogy with
'musical pitch' (which obviously suggested something like
'absolute pitch' to him) are clues which lead directly to
his poetry. Each poem is something like the conversion of
a neurosis into action; and reading his poetry with its
savage, jagged rhythms, one cannot help wondering why
Hopkins should have opposed the poetic to the religious
vocation instead of regarding them as different aspects of
the same activity. His surrender of his gift—a surrender
which he could not quite bring himself to make complete
—set up an intolerable anxiety which is reflected everywhere in his attitude to experience. Perhaps he knew how
sensual his eye and mind were, and recognized the forbidden fruit in these outbursts of sprained sexuality which
dot his note-books and his poems with splashes of bright
light. He writes:

> I have never wavered in my vocation, but I have not
> lived up to it. I destroyed the verse I had written when I
> entered the Society and meant to write no more; the
> *Deutschland* I began after a long interval at the chance sug-
> gestion of a superior, but that being done it is a question
> whether I did well to write anything else. However I shall,
> in my present mind, continue to compose, as occasion shall
> fairly allow, which I am afraid will be seldom . . . for a very
> spiritual man once told me that with things like composition
> the best sacrifice was not to destroy one's work but to leave
> it entirely to be disposed of by obedience. But I can scarcely
> fancy myself asking a superior to publish a volume of my
> verses and I own that humanly there is very little likelihood

of that ever coming to pass. And to be sure if I look at things on one and not the other I could of course regret this bitterly. But there is more peace and it is the holier lot to be unknown than to be known.

(Letters)

This heightened feeling of his own, his unique sensibility, drove him to find an appropriate expression of it in words. Observed objects, he felt, were lit with so peculiar and personal a light, that in recording his feeling about them he must try and establish the claims of his unique sensibility in forging a special technique which would carry the full weight of his emotion. It was rather the strength of his emotion that drove him in a direction of a special technique than anything else; you have the feeling that with so much power to convert into poetry Hopkins was driven to strengthen the frame of his verse in order to carry the full weight of the charge—much as an electrician will be forced to substitute thick wire for thin in order to increase the power of a current. The result of this process is that his verse-structure seems almost rubbery in its density and its plasticity. It carries a very high voltage of image and metaphor without ever giving signs of strain.

Nowhere is Hopkins sentimental, and nowhere pretty. His weakness, if he might be said to have a weakness, is excess of power. His tone of voice makes one think of a human being burning with indignation, or with shame.

> The fine delight fathers thought; the strong
> Spur, live and lancing like the blowpipe flame,
> Breathes once, and quenchèd faster than it came,
> Leaves yet the mind a mother of immortal song.
>
> (To R.B.)

And:

> Brute beauty and valour and act, oh, air, pride, plume, here
> Buckle! AND the fire that breaks from thee then, a billion
> Times told lovelier, more dangerous, O my chevalier!

No wonder of it: shéer plód makes plough down sillion
Shine, and blue-beak embers, ah my dear,
Fall, gall themselves, and gash gold-vermilion.

(*The Windhover*)

The clue to Hopkins' workshop methods is contained in his *Letters*. Here he discusses and defends his own attitudes and technique against the timid protestations of Bridges and Patmore. His poems were written, he says, for performance

> ... remember what applies to all my verse, that it is, as a living art should be, made for performance and that its performance is not reading with the eye but loud, leisurely, poetical (not rhetorical) recitation, with long rests, long dwells on the rhyme and other marked syllables, and so on.

In another place he speaks of the so-called 'sprung-rhythm' he is employing and maintains that it is 'nearest to the rhythm of prose, that is the native and natural rhythm of *speech*, the least forced, the most rhetorical and emphatic of all possible rhythms'. Both in his feeling for rhythm and in his choice of words Hopkins suggested that he was much influenced by Anglo-Saxon. He himself in one of his letters remarks that sprung rhythm exists already in Anglo-Saxon, while his selection of words betrays his taste for the short blunt Saxon words he had come across during his etymological studies. His poems are studded with words like 'pash', 'mammock', 'rival', 'sillion' and 'heft' which he had collected in the course of his studies. He was in revolt against the dreamy sentimentality of the current poetic vocabulary. 'I also cut myself off,' he writes to Bridges, 'from the use of *ere, o'er, wellnigh, what time, say not* (for *do not say*) because, though dignified, they neither belong to nor ever could arise from, or be the elevation of, ordinary modern speech.' If he was looking for the most

170

intense way of rendering his sensations he was also determined that it should be the most natural.

But to write in such an unfamiliar rhythm left him with
another problem on his hands: that of notation. His poems
should be dramatically pointed for the reader . . . 'it would
be an immense advance', he wrotes on this subject, 'in
notation (so to call it) in writing as the record of speech, to
distinguish the subject, verb, object and in general to
express the construction to the eye; as is done partly by
punctuation by everybody, partly in capitals by the Ger-
mans, more fully in accentuation by the Hebrews. And I
daresay it will come. But it would, I think, not do for me:
it seems a confession of unintelligibility. And yet I don't
know . . . Besides metrical marks are meant for the per-
former and such marks are proper in every art.' In another
letter accompanying a poem he warns Bridges: 'Take
breath and read it with the ears, as I always wish to be
read, and my verse becomes all right. . . .'

So it is that in Hopkins' verse we find the utmost
originality and sophistication of technique married to a
word-selection which is rugged and direct, and which
steers away from sentimentality and archness. That his
style contains, apart from compression, many examples of
the heightened consciousness which brings about syn-
æsthesia, is not remarkable. We have spoken of the terrific
positive charge that Hopkins' emotions carried; that these
distortions of technique came from a genuine desire to
express what he felt, and not from a preoccupation with
poetic mannerism as such, may be seen in the fact that the
very prose of his private notebooks suffers from the same
distortions. The quality which, in his verse, forced him to
speak of 'bugle-blue eggs' and describe objects as 'thunder-
purple' and 'very violet-sweet' was no less operative in his
hastily jotted notes upon natural objects and landscapes.
Thus in his notebooks we read: 'But this sober grey darkness and pale light was happily broken through by the

orange of the pealing of Mitton bells'. Colour and sound overlap and marry in a single vivid apprehension of a place or an emotion.

But if Hopkins was dissatisfied with the notation of language as not being accurate enough, he was equally dissatisfied with the existing æsthetic of poetry. He had to invent his own terms of reference to account for the particularity of his vision. His use of the two words 'inscape' and 'instress'—terms which he has nowhere explained— indicate that he wanted to widen not only the effect of language, but also the æsthetic upon which his use of it was based. The critics have devoted themselves to the task of defining what Hopkins did not himself define, with considerable relish. The common reader would do well to limit his examination of Hopkins' æsthetic to the patient work of critics, without, however, troubling himself unduly about the exact meaning of either.

In a poet so conscious of himself, of his unique gift of vision, it is not unnatural to find a desire to project this uniqueness outwards upon the world, and to feel that in his art he was expressing the essence of observed objects in the totality of their relations to time and space, rather than just painting their material shells. Hopkins was after the mysterious quiddity of things; he saw things not with his eye and mind, but with his soul, his inner essence. Consequently he felt he was penetrating behind the material jacket in which phenomena clothe themselves and reaching their essence through the power of his heightened apprehension. The eye, the mind, grammar, language, rhythm—they were all the inadequate tools of this apprehension, and in order to use them he was forced to bend them all to his will. He was a poet, and consequently rooted neckfast in the sensual apprehension of things; that he should try and align the thinking man, the metaphysician, with the other inner inhabitant who observed and recorded, is perhaps unfortunate, since many readers

will be distracted from the beauty of his work by speculations concerning his own theories about it. I mean, of
course, those readers who imagine that Hopkins' work
was constructed to illustrate a metaphysic, and not that the
metaphysic was invented in order to explain both the
feelings and the poetry which rose from them: and which
seemed strange to the author.

In a recent well-argued study of Hopkins' beliefs and
the influences which governed his writing and thinking
Dr. W. A. M. Peters, S.J., writes:

> It is with a profound admiration of Aristotle that in 1870
> he began the course of philosophical studies in the Society of
> Jesus, lasting for three complete years. We should expect that
> the philosophy taught in that Order, being that of St.
> Thomas Aquinas, would have attracted Hopkins, precisely
> because St. Thomas built his system on the philosophy of
> Aristotle. The fact, however, is that at the end of his second
> year he had transferred his loyalty to Duns Scotus.

It is in Duns Scotus, according to Dr. Peters, that we may
look for a concept which bears a close resemblance to
Hopkins' 'instress'. It is, he says, what Scotus has called
*haecceitas*—'which is the final determination of being in its
specific essence'. He adds that *haecceitas* signifies 'this-ness',
and goes on:

> Thus while in the philosophy of Aristotle and St. Thomas
> there is no separate entity which limits the universal, deter-
> mines and individualizes it, there is such a separate entity in
> the theory of Scotus: and inscape was for Hopkins its sensible
> manifestation. From this it follows that according to Scotus
> created things are immediately active in virtue of this
> separate entity, the individuating 'haecceity'; for this prin-
> ciple, being 'form', is active. In Aristotle and St. Thomas
> on the other hand things are not so immediately active, be-
> cause the individuating principle, the matter, is a passive
> principle. This theory of Scotus again confirmed Hopkins'
> vision of things as ever active.

Since Hopkins never defined either 'instress' or 'inscape' with any accuracy the field is open to speculation, and many critical theories have been put forward to explain the meaning of these terms which occur in great profusion both in his notebooks and in his letters to friends. It is doubtful whether the ordinary reader will ever get closer to the meaning of either than in this explanation of them by Dr. Peters in his painstaking and instructive study of Hopkins as a poet:

> The original meaning of 'instress' then is that stress or energy of being by which 'all things are upheld' (Hopkins' *Notebook*) and strive after continued existence. Placing 'instress' beside 'inscape' we note that the instress will strike the poet as the force that holds the inscape together; it is for him the power that ever actualizes the inscape. Further we observe that in the act of perception the inscape is known first and in this grasp of the inscape is felt the stress of being behind it, is felt its instress.

If Hopkins had been a greater poet, if he had been a 'universal' poet, it is possible that his metaphysics would have been more important to understand; as it is no reader could be blamed for accepting him purely as a poet, and accepting his poetry as an expression of a famished sensuality exploiting language in order to record its impressions of the outside world. I am deeply conscious of the fact that so far I have made no attempt to indicate what I mean by the 'universality' of the greatest poets. The truth is that I shrink from obtruding upon you the arguments of those who divide up language into two sorts: the language of 'logic' and the language of 'affect'. The distinction seems to me too narrow to be satisfying, for language at its most 'affective' seems to contain, not a logic, but a new kind of logic. The poetry which rises above categories is not nonsense, but a different kind of sense—sense without the help of standard logic, if you like.

The power of a phrase like 'the death-divining swan' lies neither in its 'logic' nor in its 'affect'. It has enough of both. It has something else, a gnomic flavour, which I do not find in Hopkins. I do not wish to denigrate the marvellous qualities of his work, but only to suggest that he belongs to a category of poet which misses greatness in the sense of 'universality'; Donne is another poet of the same kind. As a young man he wrote poems about physical love and as an old man poems about divine love. In a sense they are the same poems. For Donne as for Hopkins one feels that the brick wall surrounding his personality was too much for him to scale; he shut out all thought of the landscape outside; this is what gives his work the feeling of exhaustion and atrophy when we compare it with the ample, generous work of a 'universal' man. Neither Donne nor Hopkins ever emerged from their intellectual seclusion into that reconciliation and relaxation that we find in the later poetry of the greatest poet. From first to last they were locked in their personalities by a wilful choice of their own. They remain, with all their perfections, miniaturists; and when one considers their work as a totality reflecting their personalities one is tempted to ascribe to them something like a spiritual tone-deafness. But these strictures must seem impertinent coming from any critic, or any writer who cannot emulate a tenth part of the greatness of either. If Hopkins is not among the greatest of poets, he is greater than any poet we as a public have ever deserved.

A few remarks upon his technique should be of practical assistance to the ordinary reader of his poetry. It was not until 1882 that he began a systematic study of Old English, but for many years before he had been interested in etymology and sensitive to the need for purifying the language. It was very much a fashion of the period to dwell upon the Anglo-Saxon origins of speech—one of its aspects was the frequent naming of children after the remoter

Anglo-Saxon heroes. Among the doughtier supporters of all things Anglo-Saxon was the poet William Barnes, whose *Early England and the Saxon-English* (1869) and *Outline of English Speech-Craft* (1878) championed the use of what he thought to be purer English than that which was in use.

Barnes himself set an example by writing in a kind of purified English which is full of oddity and charm, and which might well have given Hopkins some ideas. Speaking of the degree of comparison, for example, he writes: 'These pitch-marks offmark sundry things by their sundry suchnesses', a phrase which might well have occurred in one of Hopkins' notebooks on poetry. Barnes was all for purifying English, and if he had had his way we should be calling a democracy a 'folkdom' and a butler a 'wine-thane' and a perambulator a 'push-wainling'. That Hopkins himself was sympathetic to Barnes' theories, albeit rather amused by them, there is little doubt. In one of his letters he writes:

. . . The Rev. Mr. Barnes, good soul . . . has published a *Speechcraft of English Speech*—English Grammar, written in an unknown tongue, a sort of modern Anglo-Saxon, beyond all that Furnival in his wildest Forewords ever dreamed. He does not see the utter hopelessness of the thing. It makes one weep to think what English might have been; for in spite of all that Shakespear and Milton have done with the compound I cannot doubt that no beauty in a language can make up for want of purity. . . . But the madness of an almost unknown man trying to do what the three estates of the realm together could never accomplish. He calls degrees of comparison pitches of suchness: we *ought* to call them so, but alas.

But Hopkins was not only interested in the possibilities of English. He studied Welsh, Irish and Maltese, and even the Lancashire dialect—while in letters he has referred to the Coptic and Egyptian languages and discussed philological problems concerning them. In Welsh at any rate he would have found a pattern for his verse-rhythms in the form called the *cynghanedd*. This has been defined as 'a fairly strict system of alliteration in which instead of one consonant being repeated, as in English verse, a series of different consonants is repeated in varying order.' Writing in a recent number of *Poetry London*, Tambimuttu, defending Dylan Thomas against the charge of obscurity, mentions this Welsh form as being the secret to much of Thomas's feeling for rhythm. He gives an example from Thomas's 'Blackened with birds *took* a last *look*', and points to its similarity with Hopkins' line 'The down-dugged ground *hugged* grey'.

But a good poet's work is more than the sum of his borrowings, and nobody can read Hopkins without feeling the exquisite rightness of his style, the hair-trigger accuracy and speed with which it carries flash after flash of observation and exclamation. His poetry gives a new flavour to the language, and enriches literature with a new and very personal accent.

## CHAPTER 9

# NEW SIGNATURES, NEW VOICES

THE characteristic movement of the thirties, it is said, derived much of its impetus from Marx, and more from Freud. It is still not clear, however, whether the poets of this decade actually read these two great men or, if they did, whether they assimilated them. One has the feeling in reading the poetry of this time, that the Marx-Freud influence was not a pure one—in the sense that the influence of Macchiavelli over the Elizabethans was not a pure one. In a sense the Elizabethans re-invented Macchiavelli to suit their own purposes. They did not study him closely. The general picture of what he was supposed to stand for was projected outwards into a troubled world, and the minor dramatists and writers snatched up the myth and turned it to their own uses without bothering overmuch about sources. The English Macchiavelli was by no means the same as the Italian one. Did something like this happen to Marx and Freud in the thirties?

I referred to Marxism earlier as the ugly duckling of all the philosophies which grew up under the direct influence of Scientific Materialism. Owing to its uncompromising attitude, and its cast-iron premises, it has never grown up, never to this day found an Einstein. It lags far behind physics in this respect. It is consequently more out of date than any other belief of this time looking at it from the contemporary standpoint: while its application in certain parts of the world has led to tyranny unexampled and a complete destruction of the kind of values upon which poetry can be constructed. But English

Marxism (and particularly during the thirties) was very far from the spirit of the original holy books.

The Fabians had filtered it down. It had somehow got entangled with a whole series of moral propositions about the brotherhood of man, a classless society, etc., which could not be properly related to the parent body of doctrine. The sentimentalists of the Labour Party had dragged in the Beatitudes and the Sermon on the Mount to shore up the tottering bastions of a purely *materialistic* conception of society and the individual. They borrowed the rude ethics of Christendom and rejected everything else about it in favour of a Utopian dream of a free, classless and ennobled form of society, organized on scientific principles, and expressing brotherly love.

Meanwhile the propagandists for Soviet Russia hammered away at the idea that over there (i.e. Russia) the new experiment was developing favourably and would in the end conquer the world. Some of our greatest writers lent their names to this colossal bluff, this pipe-dream which was to turn out a nightmare; scientist and economist alike harnessed their philosophy to the Marxist Juggernaut and to this day a considerable body of talented men are being dragged along in its wake.

From the time of William Morris onwards the Socialist currents had grown in force. Men like Bernard Shaw (who should have known better) lent their talents to it. Wells harped on scientific Utopias. The Webbs beatified the Soviet State. Science and Sociology and Economics alike all sprinkled holy water over the effigy of this new society.

Now Marxism as a criticism of a society which has a lot wrong with it was one thing; as an empirical theory it was all very well. But at the time it was conceived the prevailing spirit was utilitarian, agnostic and atheistic. The world was hungry for belief (as always) and the only sort of revelations seemed to be coming from Science. Hence

Marxism, though it was uncompromisingly materialistic in outlook, managed to siphon off the crippled and thwarted *religious* instincts of the later Victorians. It became an article not merely of belief, but of faith. The snowball grew to such a size that by the time we reached the thirties it had become immoral for a young poet not to be a Socialist.

The appeal of this spirit was irresistible to the middle class poet, brought up on the Wellsian fiction of Utopia; it offered him something to believe in an empty world. It also soothed his social inferiority, and above all it carried with it the approbation of those wise, wise men, the scientists (they are still at it to this day). Many of the elder men, of course, had already seen through it. Eliot confessed himself openly to be a monarchist, while other poets like Roy Campbell remained uncompromisingly reactionary in their views of man and society. But the young movement of the thirties was in reaction against Conservatism of any sort. They suspected Fascists everywhere, and were indeed alarmed when writers like Wyndham Lewis and Pound showed signs of wanting to indulge in a flirtation with foreign totalitarian countries, while the fantasies of D. H. Lawrence about a civilization ruled by heroes informed with a 'dark blood-consciousness' filled them with angry alarm.

We should not lose sight of the basic differences which underlay this quarrel; Conservatism and materialism were based on opposing philosophies. The Scientific Rationalist believed (and believes) in man's ultimate conquest of nature through science, and a new world which will shape itself out of new values. The conservative attitude roughly symbolized man who was a servant of nature, an instrument of forces which remained forever beyond his control but over which he might exert a small and tenuous influence. Man must become more responsive, more humble, not more knowledgeable, more arrogant. The Rationalist

saw Christianity as a dead and obstructing force; the Conservative believed that it enshrined truths which were forever true, in any conditions, and that the age demanded
values more than sociological fanaticisms. The one saw
society as a machine (the Scientific fallacy again); the
other as an organism which was shot through with values
that could easily be damaged and obliterated by sudden
and sweeping changes. These, then, were the basic differences of principle out of which political allegiance to one
part or another grew up. The quarrel has by no means
ended, yet it has become clear to most that neither Darwin
nor Communism offers any genuine outlet to the poetic
talent. As Robert Graves and Laura Riding write, in one
of their essays:

Communism makes no provision whatever for the poet,
but shrewdly designs his suppression. The poet who has to
endure democratic publishing methods may still find dignity
in the thought that he is not conspiring against himself, that
he merely stands for the moment as a member of a prepos-
terously large literary fellowship—the vanity of others is no
outrage to his own dignity. But the poet who surrenders to
Communism conspires in his own suppression. He consoles
himself with the thought that the physical resurrection
which is the ideal of Communism may eventually bring
about the rebirth of poetry; yet he knows that poetry is
never what will be, but always what is. He is a tired man,
in search of a long physical rest; and once he lies down on the
bed of Communism he will never rise again.

Fascism neither issues invitations nor makes any promises
to the poet, though like Communism it attempts to arouse
feelings of guilt in him towards his immediate physical
world. It gives him a stern warning not to distract the public
mind from that sense of triumph in physical existence which
it is the Fascist object to cultivate. Fascism attempts to con-
solidate as adequate reality the nation's given physical
properties; Communism, to render reality in physical terms
and create new physical values to fill out the despiritualized
universe.

So much for Marx. But what about Freud? Most of the poets of this generation claimed him as an influence, but once more one is tempted to wonder whether they had, in fact, studied him deeply, or had simply constructed a generalized picture of him as the Elizabethans did with Macchiavelli. The one exception, I would say, is Auden who at every point betrays a profound and thorough knowledge of psycho-analysis, and has acknowledged the debt to both Freud and Groddeck in the most moving terms.

The great landmark then that sticks out is the year 1930 when the poems of W. H. Auden were published. Here was a new voice of considerable power, a new technique, a new way of handling images: and in the wake of Auden came a group of fine poets which issued its first anthology *New Signatures* in 1932. Today they are all established, but it is impossible to describe the effect they made on younger writers with this, their first collective appearance. The smouldering embers of Georgian tradition burst into flame and from the cheerless hearths of papers like *The Poetry Review* the critics woke up and sharpened their battle-axes. Here was something really new, and worth attacking.

Auden was the best of these poets, and the most original from every point of view. He seemed at home in every medium—in the short, four-beat rhythm of cabaret jazz, in the ballad, and in the iambic metre with its dependence upon vowel-sounds. Even his earliest work is positively protean in its range of techniques, and the fearlessness with which it used the available contemporary subject-matter. For Eliot the introduction of a steam-engine or a city typist had been a matter of irony and disgust. Auden was less inhibited and enjoyed a greater range of human sympathy. He tried his hand at everything, from jazz-lyrics in two-four time, to free verse: and all his productions were stamped with authority and a feeling of mastery over his medium.

The subject-matter for this early poetry (a subject-matter very largely shared by the other contributors to *New Signatures* whose names are familiar to you today—Day Lewis, Stephen Spender, Louis MacNeice) was very largely social criticism. Society was breaking down into chaos, and the only hope for it was Marx. Fascism was at the doorstep and had to be fought. The new citizen, who was undergoing intellectual and social exploitation by the capitalist boss, must be warned of the dangers which beset him. Drugged with jazz and materialism, economically enslaved, he was in danger of bringing the dictator to power. How true this analysis of things was is apparent today. How inadequate the solutions presented to this problem of the human condition—is only today becoming apparent.

Yet in the first flush of Marxist enthusiasm these deeper issues (which savoured of liberalism and laisser-faire) were swept aside. But if the Marxist solution seems today to fall short of the needs of society, we must at least admit that these poets were accurate critics of the prevailing situation, at the time. Even more important than this, they were poets first, and dogmatists afterwards. In all their poetry of this period they stressed the values of the human heart, the human individual. Though at times the orthodox social doctrine came to the surface and made some of their work a little youthful and even ridiculous perhaps, yet the saving qualities of compassion and humour were always there.

In the light of all we have seen since 1930 we cannot say how far they were wrong in their analysis of society: at the most we can say that their solutions were perhaps over-optimistic. Yet these poets, each in different ways, gave us something new to work on. Auden's influence freed us from the feeling of chilly formalism and logic-chopping which we felt so strongly in the criticism of Eliot and the polemics of Lewis; he increased our feeling for the possibilities of language, showed us that poetry can be written in any form, and taught us to consider everything from the nursery-rhyme to the jazz-lyric as a proper object of study and experiment.

Spender and Day Lewis were both gifted with a romantic sensibility and a feeling for the 'emotive' value of words. They took over, in a most brilliant way, the romantic equipment of Yeats, and turned it to good account by marrying up symbols like 'rose' and 'steam-engine': we might say that in them the romantic symbol was renewed and controlled. They presented in their poems a happy marriage of old symbols in new forms. Meanwhile Louis MacNeice provided a new mixture of classical sensibility with a lazy ranging Irish technique, and a mastery over form almost as great as that of Auden.

> But those who lack the peasant's conspirators,
> The tawny mountain, the unregarded buttress,
> Will feel the need of a fortress against ideas and against the
> Shuddering insidious shock of the theory-vendors,
> The little sardine men crammed in a monster toy
> Who tilt their aggregate beast against our crumbling Troy.
>
> For we are obsolete who like the lesser things
> Who play in corners with looking-glasses and beads;
> It is better we should go quickly, go into Asia
> Or any other tunnel where the world recedes,
> Or turn blind wantons like the gulls who scream
> And rip the edge off any ideal or dream.
>
> *(Turf-Stacks)*

Eliot had been content to depict the human condition—he had dared to propose a solution; indeed it is fairly clear from *The Waste Land* that the solution lay in the reorientation of the individual and not of the collective soul. While they were aware of this, the *New Signatures* group thought the situation too critical for any but a collective change, though Auden, even in his earlier poems, did propose a 'change of heart', based upon Freud and Marx. But where Eliot depicted the twentieth century only to turn aside from it in disgust, these poets began to specify and criticize:

> The country gentry cannot change, they will die in their
>  shoes
> From angry circumstance and moral self-abuse,
> Dying with a paltry fizzle they will prove their lives to be
> An ever-diluted drug, a spiritual tautology.
> They cannot live once their idols are turned out,
> None of them can endure, for how could they, possibly,
>  without
> The flotsam of private property, pekingese and polyanthus,
> The good things which in the end turn to poison and pus,
> Without the bandy chairs and the sugar in the silver tongs
> And the inter-ripple and resonance of years of dinner-gongs?

This is from Louis MacNeice's *An Eclogue for Christmas* which contains a tremendous catalogue of the sins of the middle classes; it resembles much of the work done by the other poets along the same lines. Day Lewis was writing in the same tradition when he put out this criticism of social irresponsibility:

> Getters not begetters; gainers not beginners;
> Whiners, no winners; no triers, betrayers;
> Who steer by no star, whose moon means nothing.
> Daily denying, unable to dig:
> At bay in villas from blood relations,
> Counters of spoons and content with cushions
> They pray for peace, they hand down disaster.
>
> They that take the bribe shall perish by the bribe,
> Drying of dry rot, ending in asylums,
> A curse to children, a charge on the state.
> But still their fears and frenzies affect us;
> Drug nor isolation will cure this cancer;
> It is now or never, the hour of the knife,
> The break with the past, the major operation.

But while much of this verse was concerned with Marxist manifesto it only represented, so to speak, the top layer or belief, which each of these poets has since either modified or diluted. Poets must develop and grow if they are real poets and not hacks. All these were real poets, and it is not surprising to find that politics gradually dropped into the background to make way for the developing sensibility of each one. This does not mean that some of them did not remain Socialists. The creed was slowly qualified and diluted with other influences. Much the best of their social criticism of the thirties remains as readable, as delightful, as when it was first published, despite the fact that today Spender has openly confessed his abandonment of Marxist principle, while Auden has returned to the Anglo-Catholicism in which he was brought up.

> It's no use raising a shout.
> No, Honey, you can cut that right out.
> I don't want any more hugs;
> Make me some fresh tea, fetch me some rugs.
> Here am I, here are you:
> But what does it mean? What are we going to do?
>
> It wasn't always like this?
> Perhaps it wasn't, but it is.
> Put the car away; when life fails,
> What's the good of going to Wales?
> Here am I, here are you:
> But what does it mean? What are we going to do?

More parody than poetry, you would think, but as the poem progresses it becomes the object it is criticizing in this mockery of a jazz-tune: it runs down like an unwound gramophone—as indeed the poet believed our civilization is running down.

> In my veins there is a wish
> And a memory of fish:

When I lie crying on the floor,
It says 'You've often done this before'.
Here am I, here are you:
But what does it mean? What are we going to do?

This, then, was the main social preoccupation of the *New Signatures* group. They castigated social aimlessness, they appealed for a new order. Their work appeared to be based upon a generous social indignation. It was only natural that some of them should turn to the stage and write verse-dramas. *The Rock* and *Murder in the Cathedral* appeared in 1934 and 1935, and had aroused fresh critical interest in what had seemed, until then, to be an obsolete form. This new departure was followed by some brilliant work for the stage. Auden and Isherwood collaborated in several plays, while Stephen Spender in *Trial of a Judge* reaffirmed his faith in the workers and underlined the dangers of power politics and dictatorship. Auden and Isherwood's *The Ascent of F-6* is perhaps the most successful production by the writers of the *New Signatures* group, though many might prefer *The Dog Beneath the Skin*. For our purposes the former is more interesting since it shows less preoccupation with social conditions, and more with the problem of action and the responsibilities of the individual. There is more Freud in it and less Marx, and perhaps this is the first clear indication of Auden's personal development which carried him away from the collective solution towards an attitude of personal responsibility.

His later development, by confession, owes a good deal not only to Freud, but also to Homer Lane, Groddeck, and finally to Kierkegaard. While the volume and the quality of his verse did not diminish for an instant, one became aware of new values in it, of a new breadth of sympathy and understanding. His statement became simpler and harder, and his colouring cleaner. In his latest work, written in America, where he now lives, the social preoccupations have been almost entirely replaced by an attitude of humility and a renewed interest in the Christian values of the West, which will perhaps find one of their best interpreters in this vigorous and determined poet.

Auden may have been a romantic as far as his ideas are concerned, but his poetic technique always has been almost Aristotelean in its austerity. If you will forgive the metaphor, he strums on a very dry, a very highly strung, banjo. Spender and Day Lewis on the other hand are faced with the problem of subduing and giving shape to sensibilities which are primarily romantic—to judge by the way in which they use words. Auden has never run the risk of being sentimental. His technique is, at the most, capable of ironic compassion; but the highly spiced, highly coloured material worked into the poetry of Spender, for example, is sometimes in danger of sentimentality or weakness. How brilliantly this emotional attitude to language is controlled and governed by his technique may be seen from Spender's poetry written during the war. The subject-matter is nearly always descriptive-romantic yet the coldness with which it is framed and hung always converts it successfully into poetry. Day Lewis, faced by much the same problem, has been a little less successful. His latest work shows a gradually increasing interest in the subject-matter which the Georgians were so fond of—the English countryside. He has lost much of the bite of his social criticism without, it would appear, having gained much in the way of self-analysis and control over his medium. But with all his defects he remains today a considerable poet, as does MacNeice, who is now beginning to call upon the ancient Greeks, whom he translates and interprets so well, to assist him with his recent preoccupations about the role of the individual in society. He too has refined his technique and made it colder, while his easy colloquial gift of language has enabled him to deal with personal and emotional themes without, at any point, letting them degenerate into sentimentality. Of all these poets he confesses himself most easily and naturally in verse, and is always moving and warming to read. Auden criticizes himself, but tends to hide behind a metaphysical smoke-screen. Spender is best when least confessional. His gift is a tenderness of eye, a gift for describing and annotating experience memorably. His famous anthology-piece *The Express* is typical of this gift at its best. Recently he has tended towards a more metaphysical attitude, and his most recent verse shows that he is advancing steadily in the direction of himself. But I have said enough to show that the whole of this group have advanced from their early social criticism towards the graver preoccupations which come out of determined self-criticism and poetic honesty.

The vogue of the verse-play deserves a brief comment. Both Eliot and the *New Signatures* poets seemed to be content to let their plays be masques, containing didactic material presented expressionistically by technical tricks, like a chorus. So far only Eliot has seriously tackled the problem which lies behind the verse-play—how to accommodate it to an audience trained up on naturalistic drama, born and bred to the cinema. His own technical considerations led him to try and use a new type of poetry, geared down almost to the level of conversation. In this he was markedly successful, and in *The Family Reunion* he set out to do more. He set out to provide drama with live characters, to make his drama more than a morality play. The theme on which this drama is based is one of guilt—not Freudian guilt, to be sure, so much as original sin. The central character Harry, pursued by the Eumenides, arrives home for a reunion with his family; their relationship, and the meaning of life, death, love—and a host of other topics—are canvassed in the play with considerable profundity and in excellent verse. It is, in a sense, a modern *Hamlet*: but where *Hamlet* ends with murder, *The*

*Family Reunion* suggests another kind of solution—reintegration through a sense of spiritual responsibility. Of all the verse-plays written during this period, and even since, it is the one which most deserves to be studied seriously. Both in its manipulation of subject-matter, the use of chorus to punctuate ordinary conversation, and in the technical finish of the verse in which it is written it stands out.

There is, however, one thing missing—the creation of significant characters existing in the ambience of their actions. It is, of course, a fault all the verse-plays share today. In them a suggested line of conduct is preached, or a social or individual fault is reproved, and Eliot's play stops this side of successful special pleading. In other words, it never quite becomes a play. The characters are representative, as in a masque, of various human attitudes or passions. The result is that they do not inter-act upon one another, but each describes his interior state. Now in the best drama the meaning is *inferred* from the action. The verse-play of today explains too much. Instead of movement and drama we tend to get monologue and frieze. But this is not to denigrate the fine poetry and great craftsmanship which went into the dramas of this period. I wish to suggest only that the central problem has not been solved: which is how to marry naturalism and realism to the symbol for an audience brought up on the mechanical and naturalistic treatment of reality by the film. In this sense the verse-play is still in its experimental stage, nevertheless Eliot has boldly carried the process forward to a triumphal end in his latest play, *The Cocktail Party*, which contains beautiful simple writing with real drama, and a profound sense of metaphysical values underlying the common life of the individual. His one shortcoming is still his failure to create characters significant for what they do rather than what they *represent*.

The news that *Murder in the Cathedral* is to be filmed gives one something fresh to think about. The editing of Shakespeare for the film of *Henry V* and the recent success of *Hamlet*, lead one to hope that verse will soon find its way into cinema: for it is becoming obvious that the realistic tradition in films is becoming more and more exhausted. This wonderful medium is waiting to be refreshed from a new source. The only hope lies in symbolism at the expense of naturalistic action. We have already had bold experiments in terms of visual symbolism. The work of Cocteau and Orson Welles is an example of this; but the film has not yet married the image to symbolism in language. As an art-form it is still a moralistic shadow-play. It is in the state that drama found itself before the rise of the Elizabethan playwrights. It is a morality play. There is no reason why a poet with some experience of the cutting-room, and some feeling for the camera as a medium, should not give us dramas more moving than *Henry V.* The fact that Shakespeare has conquered the box office leads one to hope that we shall see the first verse-film by a modern poet before we die. In this context it would be worth pointing out how much the radio has gained in England by its encouragement of poetry and poets. The radio play, as developed by poets like Patric Dickinson and Louis MacNeice and Laurie Lee, is really a new form, depending of course on sound and not on vision, but at the same time exploiting an entirely new set of criteria, setting new standards. There is good hope that the film may one day grow up and follow suit.

Meanwhile, however, each of the poets of the *New Signatures* group has something new to offer us. Their development has moved away from the collective social attitude towards an individual stance. Auden has however held his place as the most important poet of his generation. The depths of his humanity, and the prodigious virtuosity of his technique are everywhere visible, even in the poetry of his middle period which is less exciting, less sensuous than the poetry he wrote before leaving for America. At the moment there is a critical conspiracy to depreciate his work, and to suggest that his most recent poetry is too intellectual and too grey in colouring to suggest creative development. This in my view is rubbish. Auden is a major poet, and with major poets we readers have to be a bit patient. We must not get restless if they deviate from what we imagine to be the true line of their development; if Auden's poetry is heavy with metaphysical cross-references today it is because he is working harder on himself than any other poet writing. And since he is a major poet, and like all major poets over-productive, we get a certain amount of backwash from his thinking. But in every line he writes the mastery, the sweep of technique, is clearly apparent. The poet may submerge here and there in the sea of his personal preoccupations; but Auden, when he chooses to surface for air, is still the greatest of his contemporaries.

His greatest gift is economy. There is hardly a wasted punch, whether he is manipulating the old ragged sixteen-syllable metre of ballad or the short clean five-foot iambic. Even in the poetry of his social-criticism period this cleanness of form was evident.

> Get there if you can and see the land you once were proud
> to own
> Though the roads have almost vanished and expresses never
> run:
> Smokeless chimneys, damaged bridges, rotting wharves and
> choked canals,
> Tramlines buckled, smashed trucks lying on their side across
> the rails.

After this general introduction to the industrial chaos of England he begins to enumerate the social attitudes and irresponsibilities which have been the cause of the trouble. I select a few verses here and there from this long ballad

to illustrate both his earlier method and the preoccupation
to illustrate both his earlier method and the preoccupations of the decade in which he began to publish.

Far from where we spent the money, thinking we could well
 afford
While they quietly undersold us with their cheaper trade
 abroad.

At the theatre, playing tennis, driving motor-cars we had,
In our continental villas mixing cocktails for a cad.

Lured by their compelling logic, charmed with beauty of
 their verse,
With their loaded sideboards whispered 'Better join us, life
 is worse.'

Perfect pater. Marvellous mater. Knock the critic down who
 dares—
Very well, believe it, copy, till your hair is white as theirs.

Shut up talking, charming, in the best suits to be had in
 town,
Lecturing on navigation while the ship is going down.

Drop these priggish ways for ever, stop behaving like a stone,
Throw the bath-chairs right away and learn to leave ourselves alone.

If we really want to live we'd better start at once to try;
If we don't it doesn't matter but we'd better start to die.

Auden's debt to the psychologist is perhaps most apparent in the way he uses the nursery rhyme. In the poetry
of de La Mare and Edith Sitwell we get a preoccupation
with the childish sensibility, but it is purely sensuous.
Auden uses a different technique. For him the childish
symbols are essentially reflections from a world of terror
and mystery; and his trick of personifying abstractions is a
development from his earlier method of introducing

Jungian and Freudian symbols—'hump-backed scissor-man' and the other images belonging by rights only to Struwelpeter and Lewis Carroll. For de La Mare and Edith Sitwell the poetry of childhood is still what our Victorian grandfathers would call 'wholesome'. There is little to terrify us about it. It is essentially a period of innocence. But Auden belongs to the generation which acknowledged the concept of the libido, and realized that our earliest impressions of guilt and terror were supposed to be buried in our childhood. For him childhood is an age of responsibility and preoccupation. And even now, in his latest poetry, he gives his personified metaphysical abstractions the mythological touch of childish symbols, half-understood and almost wholly frightening:

> Then he harrowed hell,
>   Healed the abyss
> Of torpid instinct and trifling flux,
> Laundered it, lighted it, made it lovable with
> Cathedrals and theories; thanks to him
>   Brisker smells abet us,
> Cleaner clouds accost our vision
>   And honest sounds our ears.
> For he ignored the Nightmares and annexed their ranges,
> Put the clawing Chimaeras in cold storage,
> Berated the Riddle till it roared and fled,
>   Won the Battle of Whispers,
> Stopped the Stupids, stormed into
> The Fumblers' Forts, confined the Sulky
> To their drab ditches and drove the Crashing
>   Bores to their bogs,
>   Their beastly moor.
>                     (*The Age of Anxiety:* 1948)

Apart from their individual books of verse and from their anthologies, these poets were consistently represented in the pages of *New Verse* (1933-39) which for several years held the interest of the verse-reading public by its skilful editing, and the high standard of its contributions. After T. S. Eliot's *Criterion* (1922-39) this was perhaps the most important periodical of the day. While it did not print the older and more established poets it was responsible for bringing many new names to the public eye. Among these we should mention two poets who did not belong to any particular group, and apparently did not support any political or social movement: Dylan Thomas and George Barker. And during the same period we should signal the emergence of two important women poets, Kathleen Raine and Anne Ridler. With the addition of one more name—that of William Empson—we should end this brief review of the thirties.

## CHAPTER 10

# POETRY IN THE THIRTIES

DYLAN THOMAS and William Empson deserve to be
read side by side, not because of any similarity but because
of their radical differences of approach. Both are difficult
poets, but the reasons that make them difficult lie in
opposite corners, so to speak. Contrasts as extreme as this
are worth examining together, for they illuminate each
other far more clearly than any similarity of temperament
or technique could do. Yet the superficial ambiguity of
their work might, at first blush, suggest a common attitude
or a common approach.

Thomas, a Welshman, is less interested in making his
poetry a means of communicating ideas than Empson. He
is attempting a compression even greater than that of Hopkins, squeezing up his material and his rhythm until his
poems resemble mere ideograms for thought or emotion.
His poetry is the poetry of sensuality and incantation, and
while he can glance sideways at the verse of Hopkins
which influenced it there is another, smokier flavour in it,
which it would not be wrong to think of as peculiarly
Welsh. Thomas is a prophet, and whatever he touches
reminds one of the Bible and of the Blake of the Prophetic
Books.

> And I must enter again the round
> Zion of the water bead
> And the synagogue of the ear of corn
> Shall I let pray the shadow of a sound
> Or sow my salt seed
> In the least valley of sackcloth to mourn

The majesty and burning of the child's death.
I shall not murder
The mankind of her going with a grave truth
Nor blaspheme down the stations of the breath
With any further
Elegy of innocence and youth.

This is an example of his later manner in which rhythm and compression have loosened in order to carry the sense more clearly; but in his first volume and for several years before the war Thomas was operating in a different key, and employing a compression of symbols which reminded one of Joyce's *Finnegan's Wake*: for while the connecting line of direct statement was absent, each image was raised to its full symbolic power. This squeezing up, together with the rugged but always controlled rhythms gave his verses roughness of surface and terrific impact, though one had to dig with both hands for the meaning.

The force that through the green fuse drives the flower
Drives my green age; that blasts the roots of trees
Is my destroyer.
And I am dumb to tell the crooked rose
My youth is bent by the same wintry fever.

Yet the meaning was always there, even if at times it seemed to be snowed up with images. In the latest poetry Thomas has written he has modified his technique to allow it to carry simpler meanings more clearly; but his construction and sound-values remain. His voice is an unmistakeable one and his influence over the younger poets nearly as strong as Hopkins' influence over his own early verse. His ability to raise symbols to a higher power by the ambiguity of their position in a line of poetry is a gift which no one else today shares. One has the impression in reading Thomas that he sees the world in a new way— through a microscope. His symbols reach back into the unconscious, into the ¡jungle of their primitive origins, while his use of sound gives them almost brutal force when they reach the ear. It is not clear how much he is indebted to the psychologists but an examination of his marriage of matter to manner suggests that, like Joyce, he has made good use of the work done by Jung on the archetypal symbol.

Empson is the Chinaman in our midst. His poems are carefully constructed wholes, always based upon an exacting metaphysical ideal of communication—which comes no doubt from his careful study of linguistics. His critical volume *Seven Types of Ambiguity* (1930) is a valuable help in gauging his attitude to verse. But where Thomas is sensual and romantic, Empson is an intellectual poet using ambiguity only because his metaphysics do not lend themselves to simple statement. Thomas is concerned primarily with the impact of his images upon the reader's subconscious; Empson appeals to his reason. His ironic despair springs, no doubt, from his realization of how limited the semantic field is to the observer. Yet his work as a critic has been of the utmost value with its insistence upon careful analysis of models, and deliberate interpretation of obscurity, while his own poetry is a most honourable illustration of his principles. If I referred to him as a Chinaman it was to try and indicate that his profound knowledge of linguistics and philosophy had led him into a philosophic position which we might describe as one of compassionate detachment. But his real contribution to poetry is in the logical way he has disturbed syntax to force multiple meanings upon the structure of words. He is a real space-time poet. Thomas is often genuinely obscure—perhaps even to himself. His poems are aimed at you like loaded sand-bags. Empson is only obscure because the pattern of his syntax is working overtime, to carry multiple meanings and sharply opposed contrasts.

Those thorns are crowns which, woven into knots,
Crackle under and soon boil fools' pots;
And no man's watching, wise and long,
Would ever stare them into song.

Thorns burn to a consistent ash, like man;
A splendid cleanser for the frying pan:
And those who leap from pan to fire
Should this brave opposite admire.

The contrast presented by these two poets, both difficult to read, is a contrast between the metaphysical and the prophetic. In both cases their recent work indicates a modification of technique in favour of statement. Empson's latest poetry shows a less exacting attention of detail and far less conceit (in the technical sense): while Thomas is turning his sound and fury outwards, and persuading it to assist and not to dominate his meanings. Both poets have been enriched by this relaxation of principle, and their work has become fuller of human qualities.

The case of George Barker is different; his problems have been rather like those which Yeats faced and so successfully surmounted in his last glorious poems. Barker is occupied with the task of bringing shape and order to a temperament which is essentially romantic, and a feeling for words which is sensual and musical. He is a master of vowel-sounds, and his poetry is as delicately and richly coloured as the early poetry of Keats, with whom he shares certain superficial resemblances. His strong suit is not statement but music and invocation. At his best his poetry is the poetry of sorcery and spells; and his use of musical pattern and internal rhyme have won him a well-deserved reputation which is, by now, established and firm. He, too, is busy growing, taming his romantic sensibility which often leads him to commit excesses in his verse—too facile invocation is one of his sins, and a tendency towards euphuism another. But his *Pacific Sonnets* and his post-war poems suggest that he is exercising greater control over his material without letting it lose either colouring or emotion.

Of the two women poets mentioned, both laid the foundations to their present reputation during the thirties though it would be safe to say that until the founding of *Poetry London* (1939) by Tambimuttu they did not enjoy a public platform. Yet they were both well-known. Kathleen Raine's best work, however, has been published since the war. It is the work of a crystal-gazer, very firmly shaped and very simple and moving. It does not offer very great complexity to the general reader, although its subject-matter is largely religious and mystical. Its grace and point give it weight: not the overpowering weight of an Edith Sitwell who fashions her work from whole ingots of gold: but the weight of gold-dust, shall we say, or quartz crystals, or the dust of diamonds?

Anne Ridler, no less meticulous and fastidious, chooses a larger if simpler canvas and a bigger brush. Her themes are everyday ones and they are always handled with remarkable honesty and craftsmanship. She does not go in for invocation and rhetoric but for scrupulous clarity of statement. She does not exclaim and point, and the emotional line which runs through her poetry is always adult and severe. She is new in the sense that she dares to be a woman in her poetry—which women usually do not. They prefer to be saints or mystics. Kathleen Raine, for example, is a remote descendant of Alice Meynell and Christina Rossetti. It is much harder to write about children and marriage and the architecture of your personal life, yet these form the subject-matter of nearly all Anne Ridler's poetry. And she handles them with a wonderful feeling for form and colour and rhythm. She never tries to appear what she is not, and she never strains her technical equipment. Everything she does has finish and grace. She is too fastidious to strike attitudes.

These, then, are the main talents of the thirties which

lay outside the immediate orbit of the *New Signatures* Group, though in some cases *New Verse* gave them representation.

But it should not be forgotten that throughout this period the elder poets were exercising their influence upon the younger. Yeats, whose last poems influenced nearly all the young poets of this generation, only died in 1939, having finally triumphed in the long and bitter struggle he had waged with himself—a struggle to subdue a romantic and richly Irish sensibility, which seemed always prepared to dissolve his poems in seas of symbolism.

From the beginning of his life to the end he hated science and rationalism, and took refuge from it in mythology and religion. At his best he was always a major poet, even in his worst period; but the defects of style against which he struggled were the result of a passionate and colourful temperament with its bias for romantic symbolism. In his last period he underwent a complete transformation of manner. It was not that he adopted a new style of writing, but all at once the philosophic preoccupations which obsessed him sank to the bottom of his verse, and he began to write with a poignance and lucidity such as is given to few poets to achieve. He married art to emotion with complete success and more than fulfilled the promise of his Tennysonian youth.

That is no country for old men. The young
In one another's arms; birds in the trees,
—Those dying generations—at their song;
The salmon-falls, the mackerel-crowded seas,
Fish, flesh or fowl, commend all summer long
Whatever is begotten, born, and dies.
Caught in that sensual music all neglect
Monuments of unageing intellect.

An aged man is but a paltry thing,
A tattered coat upon a stick, unless
Soul clasp its hands and sing, and louder sing

For every tatter in its mortal dress,
Nor is there singing school but studying
Monuments of its own magnificence;
And therefore I have sailed the seas and come
To the holy city of Byzantium.

We might imagine that these utterances come from a latter-day Ulysses or Gerontion in order effectively to examine the general theme—which is once more old age, death, and the thoughts which are manufactured in an old man's mind when he contemplates these subjects in the light of his own destiny. We can see at once that the wheel has turned full circle again; there is a new and beautiful integration of spirit behind this sort of utterance which tells us of doubt conquered and knowledge assimilated. The preoccupations of Gerontion have been purged in the acceptance of a new knowledge, a new way of feeling.

After his death in January 1939 Auden wrote his *In Memory of W. B. Yeats*, one of the most moving and beautiful poems, which summed up the feeling of his whole generation when they heard the news. In it he says:

For poetry makes nothing happen: it survives
In the valley of its saying where executives
Would never want to tamper; it flows south
From ranches of isolation and the busy griefs,
Raw towns that we believe and die in; it survives,
A way of happening, a mouth.

This is the most effective answer to the critic with his sterile apparatus of 'influence' and 'tendency' and his absurd chronological formula which I fear that I am imitating all too closely. Yeats' death set a term to the poetry of the oldest generation. He enjoyed a tremendously long and productive working life, consistent all the way through for steady development. Already a great poet before the turn of the century, he did not get stuck in his tradition, but carefully and thoroughly examined newer techniques. He was never ashamed to learn—and his last poems with their cold yet sensuous colouring showed his debt to the verse of the twenties. He had learned, with its help, to control and bind his own poetry more tightly, to give his emotion an almost sculptural solidity of form without losing poignance. Though his earliest work often formed a stand-by for the Georgian anthologists, his latest poems were technically very much of their period—for the really great poet is always absolutely modern by what he has to say and not by how he says it.

No less remarkable in the same period was the development shown by Edith Sitwell. Her first collected volume was published in 1930. It was full of fantasies and grotesques, of sharply contrasted verbal effects, but the subject matter was largely childhood reminiscences and nursery-forms. In this she showed great technical mastery, though at times the verse-forms seemed rather brittle and deliberately over-embroidered.

> Baskets of ripe fruit in air
> The bird-songs seem, suspended where,
>
> Between the hairy leaves, trills dew,
> All tasting of fresh green anew.
>
> Ma'am, I've heard your laughter flare
> Through your waspish-gilded hair. . . .

No verse of this period was so highly coloured and yet at the same time unromantic; reading her poetry was like biting into a sour apple. No poet worked with such deliberation in laying down her patterns of images, and arranging her vowel-schemes to her own taste. But while her work was rich in elaboration and technique it sometimes seemed lacking in content; it was as if the poetess

was content to decorate rather than to express herself. Yet
it was polished and carefully constructed decoration,
though sometimes ruined by excesses and experiments.

> From each elephantine trunk
> The waterfalls rear. Myrrhine shrunk,
> And now the barber zephyr curls
> Black cornucopias of pearls.
>
> Upon the dressing-table, heat
> Is flaunting like a parakeet,
> And in the street, dust-white and lean,
> Two black apes bear her palanquin.
>
> Through the shutters see those apes'
> Eyes like green and golden grapes.
> Their falsetto voices made
> A false simian serenade. . . .

The nursery rhyme, the taste for the baroque image,
the marriage of unlikely nouns and adjectives—these were
the striking things about her verse that influenced so many
of her younger contemporaries. Though the bulk of the
verse published in her *Collected Poems* in 1930 had been
written in the previous decade, her reputation followed
more slowly, and it was the thirties which really begun
to value her work and its true merits.

In the next decade, however, a tremendous change
took place, and during the war years Edith Sitwell took a
step forward which carried her into the forefront of English
letters. Much that was playfully and wilfully decorative
disappeared from her verse; keeping the richness of her
technique she increased its sombreness, and relaxed her
strictness in order to put the decoration at the service of
the content. She became a prophetess instead of a Harle-
quin. There was nothing brittle about this new work,
though it owed much to the years of experiment and

practice which preceded it. It was new as all great poetry is new. But her voice was hoarse and passionate where it had once been shrill and cynical; it was poetry straight from the tripod this time. Still using the old technique of alternating short and long lines, with its suspicion of free verse, she tightened and accentuated the form, and hammered home her meanings in sounds like nails. Today she is at the height of her fame, and we would not be wrong to consider her sharing the universal respect and admiration which T. S. Eliot enjoys. Of the four poets who influenced the generation of Auden, two are alive and two dead. Hopkins and Yeats are dead: Eliot and Edith Sitwell alive.

The outbreak of the war in 1939 sets up a convenient milestone at which we should perhaps call a halt. As we get nearer to our own times the field of poetry broadens out and becomes more diffuse, more complex, fuller of details. How many of these details will ultimately prove to be irrelevant we cannot say. Accurate criticism, if there is such a thing, is essentially an affair of long-sightedness. Objects too close to us must inevitably appear out of focus when we look at them: and in a survey of this kind, which cannot claim to be more than a brief introduction, one must be prepared for injustices. I do not think that they can be helped.

We have been trying to follow the great main current of a new tradition in writing. There are many unexplored backwaters, many tributaries of the main stream, which have not been explored in detail. The Georgian tradition is one. The poetry of this tradition is a mixture of arcadianism and quietism; its roots lie perhaps in the pantheism of Wordsworth. In form and content it is essentially romantic, but at its best—in the strictness of Edward Thomas' verses—it reaches a very high mark. It is also representative of something very near to the spirit of the English people. It continues to flourish side by side with the main tradition and we could, without straining interpretation, trace a direct line of descent through Drink-water, Masefield and de La Mare: through Edmund Blunden, Richard Church and W. H. Davies: to the fastidious and lovely workmanship of Andrew Young and Clifford Dyment. It implies no disrespect for this vigorous tradition that we have not examined it in great detail; the reason is that these poets present fewer difficulties in technique than those we have mentioned. They are not straining after new interpretations of themselves.

There remain other omissions. I have not mentioned those poets who are already fully formed and mature, and who are still waiting for the public response that their talent merits: Bernard Spencer and Vernon Watkins come to mind in this context. I have not mentioned those whose talent is still ripening, but who instead of the customary 'early promise' have given us already some very recogniz-able and solid achievements—Terence Tiller, Roy Fuller and Laurie Lee.

Lastly I have not mentioned the war-poets of 1939, be-cause I am unable to ·judge their value correctly at this range. The glamour of dying young still casts a halo round the heads of writers like Alun Lewis, Sidney Keyes and Keith Douglas. How much of what they left us will be considered a permanent contribution we cannot tell. We only know today that we can find in them a moving expression of the war generation's hopes and preoccupa-tions.

But if we have been unjust to some who merited more study and analysis it was in order to try and preserve the clear outlines and sober form of a general thesis: that poetry is only one dialect in the general language of ideas, and that poetry today reflects the anxieties and triumphs visible in many different fields of knowledge, philosophy, physics and psychology. Of course great poetry is every-where outside the range of such futile categories as we critics put up around it. But a generalized knowledge of the preoccupations of the twentieth century is essential today if we wish to understand why language has been pushed so far out of shape, and used in such odd ways. The revolution in ideas, both about the outer world (physics, cosmology) and about the world of the self (the ego) is clearly reflected in the technique of modern poetry, and can help us to elucidate its shifting apprehensions and attitudes. Dylan Thomas is more easily comprehensible to the critic who has read Jung, than to one who is only anxious to trace his influences in Edith Sitwell and Hopkins; the one can examine the poet's intentions, the other stops short over the idiosyncrasies of his technique.

Though we have stopped short at 1939 we have allowed two of the most significant poets of the day to overstep this mark. Eliot's *Quartets* and Edith Sitwell's poems written during the war are too important to be penned up behind the brick wall of the chronological method.

There are a number of fine poets who deserve our careful study and whom I have been obliged to jettison in order to keep these lectures within an agreed limit. In almost every case they are poets who have founded no schools and whose place in modern writing has been earned by a direct personal vision. It would be impossible not to mention the spare, satirical and vivid poems of Robert Graves, and the finely-spun metaphysical essays of Edward Muir. I trust my neglect of them will be forgiven by their admirers among whom I number myself.

As for the younger poets, they can wait until we are more certain of the values they express. For those too impatient to wait, and too anxious to predict what the future of verse is likely to be, we should recommend the files of *Poetry: London* (edited by Tambimuttu) and the pages of *New Writing* (edited by John Lehmann) which contain much of the best work of the late thirties and the early forties. Beyond this point there is no need for us to go, unless it be to mention the conquests of the London stage by the verse-plays of Christopher Fry, which is another remarkable phenomenon of the times.

Poetic development is an unknown quantity and will presumably always be so. After a poem has occurred it is an easy matter to find it a logical development of earlier tendencies. But it is impossible to predict—and more particularly when the field is as crowded as the one we are examining. There are a number of dark horses coming up on the outside which look as if they will finish in style. David Gascoyne, F. T. Prince and Ronald Bottrall come to mind in this context. But there are others: and such distinctions as we would be able to make today would prove false in the light of their future development. What could be predicted for the future development of poets like John Betjeman, John Lehmann, Paul Dehn, G. S. Fraser?

'I think,' wrote Yeats before his death, 'England has had more good poets from 1900 to the present day than during any period of the same length since the early seventeenth century.' We will have to leave it to Time to sort them out and group them for us; but Time is the slowest critic of us all.

# NOTES

## CHAPTER I

*Siphnophora:* this animal I encountered in the pages of Marais, the South African naturalist; modern science, however, claims that the description he gives of it is inaccurate. Nevertheless, I have let it stand for the sake of the analogy.
*Sherwood Taylor:* article printed in *The Listener.*

## CHAPTER 2

*Francis J. Mott:* his books are privately printed and expensive. They can be obtained from John Watkins, Bookseller, 21 Cecil Court, Charing Cross Road, London. I have found the most suggestive to be *The Universal Design of the Œdipus Complex* and *The Universal Design of Birth.*

## CHAPTER 3

*Freud:* These quotations come from a selection of essays written towards the end of his life.

## CHAPTER 4

A critic has complained that such detailed treatment of Groddeck makes me unfair to Freud, Jung, Adler, etc. It is true that Groddeck does not enjoy as wide a reputation; nevertheless he is of interest to me because his equating of mind and body does, in the medical field, roughly what Einstein has done in the realm of physics with the concepts of space and time.

CPSIA information can be obtained
at www.ICGtesting.com
Printed in the USA
BVHW01s0049061217
502048BV00012B/102/P